IT IS CONSCIOUSNESS THAT IS SEARCHING

Tribhuvanatha dasa

Published & Printed by HKF Press (ISKCON Festivals UK)
Registered UK Charity no. 259649

Printed in the United Kingdom

For orders, suggestions or for more information about the subject matter please contact: tribhuvanatha.book@gmail.com

Based on the spoken word of Tribhuvanatha dasa
Book production by Sandipani Muni Krishna dasa
Editing and proofreading by Citra Lila devi dasi

For more information please visit:

- hkfest.org
- facebook.com/harekrishnafestivalsuk
- centres.iskcon.org
- krishna.com

CONTENTS

DEDICATION

This book is dedicated to our spiritual master, His Divine Grace A.C. Bhaktivedanta Swami Prabhupada (Founder-Acharya of the International Society for Krishna Consciousness) who gave us this spiritual knowledge.

PREFACE

This book is a humble attempt to share small gems of the teachings of His Grace Tribhuvanatha dasa. He was known by many as a man of spiritual strength, character, and as a teacher or a *guru* both in people's personal life and to communities. He was a man of great spiritual insight and made valuable contributions around the world by his lectures, projects and teachings. He was a dear disciple of *guru,* His Divine Grace A.C. Bhaktivedanta Swami Prabhupada. More information about his life is provided at the end of this book.

The book is a selection of excerpts of the philosophical discourses he gave over the years. They have been gently and carefully edited for the sake of readability. For all of these lectures, the original full audio is available for free online on our website. We hope this work will constitute an inspirational and introductory philosophical book to its readers, presenting the wise, sharp and witty words of Tribhuvanatha Prabhu. We hope to make Bhakti Yoga more accessible to the world through this book. Ultimately, this book is a tribute to Srila Prabhupada.

INTRODUCTION

AT THE LONDON SCHOOL OF PHARMACY, UK - 18 FEBRUARY 1999

The Vedic literature teaches us that consciousness comes from the superior energy and matter comes from the inferior energy. The superior and inferior energies are two completely separate and distinct energies. We find in the modern world, that the emphasis of scientific study is based upon the principle of material existence or the inferior energy. However, the emphasis given in the Vedas is on the study of the transcendental or superior energy, known in Sanskrit as *parabrahman*. *Para* means superior, and *brahman* means spirit. The Vedas explain that the spiritual entity belongs in the eternal spiritual atmosphere and has an eternal relationship with the Supreme Spirit, Krishna. The quality of the individual spirit is that it has individual consciousness which is signified or manifested in life symptoms. One of those chief life symptoms is independence. The misuse of independence brings the living entity into an environment in which he can exercise his illusory desire to be a completely dominant entity.

The difference between the superior and inferior energy is that the superior energy is immeasurable, whereas the inferior energy is limited, temporary and measurable. When the living entity misuses his independence to forget God, he comes into the material world and takes on a materially designated body. In that designated body he exercises his freedom - which is the sum and substance of the law of what we call *karma*. The law of *karma* is the science of action and reaction; it is played out through living entities having an individual choice to act according to their desire.

That desire is controlled by higher nature. In other words, material nature, being under the control of God, is more powerful than the individual living entity. God is still manifested in the material world, in his separated energy, which is called *maya* or matter. When the living entity has become exhausted in his artificial desire to be independent of God or to be an independent conscious controller, then he can give up that artificial consciousness and realise that he is an eternal servant of God. That servitude between the individual living entity and the complete whole entity God is called Krishna consciousness or Bhakti Yoga.

1: IT IS CONSCIOUSNESS THAT IS SEARCHING

A LECTURE GIVEN AT A PUBLIC FESTIVAL

The Krishna conscious philosophy is very ancient, it's not something new. It is many thousands of years old, over five thousand years old. It is also called Vedanta or Vedic knowledge. It is not Hinduism. Many people think Hinduism is a religion. Actually, no philosophy in the world mentions the word *Hindu*. It doesn't exist. Hinduism is taken from the pronunciation of the Pathans or the Afghanis when they attacked India. They started the use of the word *Hindu*. Indus is a valley. They had a different pronunciation, so that's where the word Hindu came from. The word *veda* means truth. Vedic philosophy is not a religion as many people think - in the normal sense of the word - because religion means a type of faith. Faith is changeable. You can change your faith because faith is generally based upon a certain degree of information. And information in the material world tends to increase or decrease, it tends to change since it's not coming from the absolute plane.

The first principle of knowledge is to understand *why* we need to know something. That should be the first consideration when acquiring knowledge. If every one of us were perfect - and that is what everybody strives for - then we all would have perfect knowledge. Everybody is striving to perfect their knowledge. Nobody takes pleasure in being ignorant. Actually, ignorance is not bliss. Ignorance is the cause of all types of miseries!

This search or quest for knowledge is a very important thing because it is the fundamental difference between humans and animals. Other than that, man could be termed as an animal, as humans have animal propensities. The animal has a different type of body to us, and we might say that some animals are inferior but we also see that in many ways animals are superior to us. We are comparatively limited in our eyesight, whereas some animals have very good eyesight. Just like the hawk or the eagle, they can see a very small mouse or a rabbit from a very high distance. We can see also that the bird has the incredible ability to fly. If you went to the top of a twenty-story building and leapt off, you'd come sailing down to the floor at great speed, whereas the bird feels no fear in jumping off a very high building. For the bird, it's a very pleasurable experience because he has the ability to manoeuvre in the air, so in that sense he's superior. We can't fly in the air and so we have to build a big, very awkward, cumbersome machine. You can't exactly have a jumbo jet parked outside of your door if you want to fly.

By studying nature and our surroundings we can understand the difference between humans and animals. The *Bhagavad-gita* describes that the animals have certain propensities. The animal has the propensity to eat, and we also have the propensity to eat. The animal also has the propensity to sleep, we also have the propensity to sleep. The animal also engages himself in mating and defending and we do too.

There's a very nice story about a camel and a scorpion that wanted to cross a river. The scorpion was unable to cross the river because the water was obviously too deep for it. But the camel was able. The scorpion wanted to ride on the hump of the camel because he knew that by getting on his hump he would be able to cross over the river. The camel said to the scorpion, 'Well if I take you on my back, you may sting me and then I'll die'. But the scorpion said, 'No, no, if I sting you, then you'll sink and I'll die also. So I promise I won't sting you'. So the camel agreed. Then halfway across the river, sure enough, the scorpion stung the camel and as they were sinking, the camel said to him, 'Oh! Why have you done that?' and the scorpion said, 'I couldn't help myself, it's my nature!'

So as this story explains, everybody has their conditioned nature. We say, 'Oh, that's his nature, he's like that'. But we don't really understand the mystery of nature. There is a great experience in studying nature. We can see that everyone is embodied and conditioned by their body. I have a limited ability to see and to hear. I have a limited ability of my sense of touch and sense of taste and smell.

The *Bhagavad-Gita* is a great science that explains everything about nature. Not only does it explain everything about nature, but it goes on to explain what its cause is. It doesn't take a lot of intelligence to observe that everything has a cause behind it. If you see a wonderful motor car, you may say, 'I wonder who designed that? I wonder which company manufactured that particular car.' So any particular item may be a wonderful display, but there must be a brain behind it.

It's stupidity to say that something simply manifests itself by accident because we have no experience that something has been manufactured by accident. Many scientists say the universe occurred by an accident. They have so many theories to try to explain how everything comes accidentally by a chemical explosion or atomic explosion. But we have no experience of something wonderful coming from an accident.

I always use the example, if you were speeding down the M1 motorway at five hundred miles an hour and you had an incredible crash, you wouldn't wake up in Hawaii on the beach with beautiful palm trees and the sun and the sea. Here is a tremendous accident but what is the result? You'll probably be splattered all over the motorway.

If the universe began by accident, then we'd all be going around having accidents. If we can produce such a wonderful creation by accident, then accidents must be a very good thing. We should all be going around having explosions because if explosions produced us and all of this variety, the fruits on the trees, and all of these wonderful different species, then it would only make sense that the bigger the explosion, the better the creation is going to be. But in reality, it is not so. In other words, anything which is brainless usually ends up in chaos.

The reality is quite the opposite. Any intelligent man can see that anything that happens is all going on by some cause. Even scientists admit that behind every effect there is an equal cause. So if we're intelligent enough to understand there are cause and effect, we must try and understand that behind the universe, behind us and the body there is some cause, and that is the real purpose of knowledge.

Knowledge means to discriminate, to make distinctions. An animal, on account of his lower development of consciousness, cannot do so. The whole Vedic civilization is based upon the study of consciousness. That's why we call it the International Society for Krishna Consciousness, because consciousness is the predominant feature of life. If I am conscious in my body that means life is present. There is the manifestation of intelligence, the mind and the senses. But when there is unconsciousness, then I can leave, I can die. Death is when there is no longer any presence of consciousness. Consciousness is the important thing. Matter itself is being moved by the presence of consciousness.

You may buy a wonderful car but unless the driver gets in and turns the key, that car will never go anywhere. Even if this room was one big computer unless the scientist comes and operates the switches there would be no activity. That computer will lie there for millions of years and rot away. In the same way, the mechanical car or anything else will never do anything unless there is the presence of consciousness. Consciousness is the single most important factor in life because it is consciousness that is searching.

I'm conscious that in this life I want to be happy. And I am conscious that there is a superior meaning to life. The Vedas explain that the so-called evolution of species is the evolution of consciousness. Consciousness manifests itself in different forms of life. This process is the transmigration of the body through various species. Each species represents a particular type of manifestation of consciousness, through the sensual body.

This is described very nicely in the *Bhagavad-Gita*, that the body is a field of activity. We all have a body, but what do we do with the body? We act. It wouldn't be much good having a body if you kept it hanging on a coat hanger in the cupboard, would it? If you said, 'I've got a wonderful body but I'm going to keep it in the cupboard and do nothing', there's no use. The body has to be active. Why? Because consciousness is eternally active. Consciousness is the spiritual presence of the soul within the body.

We have to understand the difference between matter and spirit. There is a very clear definition of the distinction between the two. Unless one can discriminate between matter and spirit, one cannot go beyond the animal platform. That is the one distinction between ourselves and animals. We can distinguish between matter and spirit. The animal does not care about the difference between matter and spirit. All it cares about is satisfying the immediate demands of the senses. A tiger is allowed to attack another animal for its food. You never find a policeman going out into the African jungle and arresting a tiger because they saw it attacking and killing a young deer or something. They know that animals act according to their nature.

There are no laws regulating animals. You don't find a dog up for arrest in court because he was trying to have sex with another dog. We know that animals are unable to discriminate. They are completely under the control of the lower energy of the body. But we see that the human being has a higher development of consciousness. Why? Because he can discriminate between the body and the self. And this is the beginning of real knowledge. Real education means to understand *aham brahmasmi*, I am *brahman* (spirit), I am not made of matter. Matter is a dead, inanimate substance. And without the presence of the soul in matter, there is no activity.

We often see that when someone is dying the doctor says, 'Oh, he's slipping away'. Then they say, 'He's dead', or 'He's gone'. But where has he gone? He's in the room. He's lying there on the bed. How can you say he's gone? Where has he gone? The doctor says, 'No, he's no longer there'. But the body is there! His eyes, his ears, the hair, his arms are there, his legs are there. Everything is there, so where has he gone? And who is this 'he'? The man may be called John Smith. But John Smith is still there. What has gone? Consciousness has gone.

Consciousness is described in the *Bhagavad-Gita*. Krishna says *deho 'smin yatha dehe kaumaram yauvanam jara*, that 'As the embodied soul continually passes, in this body, from boyhood to youth to old age, the soul similarly passes into another body at death. The self-realized soul is not bewildered by such a change', because he knows by realisation, that the body is only a temporary manifestation. Just like this young boy here. I don't know what his age is, but fifty years from now, his body will be different. He probably won't even remember being here.

The activities of the material body are all a temporary manifestation. All of us have been three years old. Now does that mean that if I showed you a photo of you three years old, that you would say that is what you look like now? Even though it is you, you couldn't get a passport with your three-year-old photo. You could say to the passport officer, 'No, this is me!' But they would say, 'It doesn't look anything like you'. You can argue, 'No, that was me'. What does it mean, 'That was me'? Is it you or was it you? That's what I used to look like. But now I look completely different.

The body we had when we were a six-month-old baby is different from the body we have now. Scientifically speaking, the body changes cell-by-cell within eight to ten years. That means all of you in this room have already reincarnated into another body. People say, 'Oh I don't believe in transmigration, I don't believe in reincarnation', but everyone in this room has changed their body completely. You may say, 'But it still feels like me'. Yes, the consciousness is identifying with that body and on account of that strong identification, he feels so.

The Vedas explain that there is the gross external body and then there's the subtle body consisting of mind, intelligence and false ego. Krishna says in *Bhagavad-Gita* that this false ego is a fool because he thinks he is the body, *ahankara vimudhatma. Ahankara* means 'false ego'. This attachment that we have to the body is also there in the animal. The animal is thinking, 'I am a dog'. He barks and runs after other dogs, acting in a very predetermined way. Predetermined by what? By higher authority.

Our bodies are made of matter which is described as the inferior energy of the Supreme Creator. Matter is also described in the Vedas as *maya. Maya* means 'that which is not' or 'illusion'. The manifestation appears to be a reality but has no existence on account of its non-permanent nature. The soul on the other hand, is eternal. Krishna says, *mamaivamso jiva-loke jiva-bhutah sanatanah*, that the living entities are fragmented portions of Krishna. Each one of us is a fragmental portion of the Absolute Truth. As stated in the Isopanisad, *om purnam adah purnam idam*, that each portion is *purnam*, complete. The Supreme Absolute Truth is the Supreme Complete. That's why in every one of us, there is the desire to become complete.

If I give you a choice between two drinks - the first is an ambrosial nectar, a wonderful drink that by drinking it, you will become eternal. Not only will it make you full of happiness but also full of ecstasy - in so much ecstasy that you'd be rolling around the floor. It is an eternal happiness. Not like the happiness when you go to the pub and roll on the floor and then when you wake up the next day with a headache. This ecstasy is eternal and it always increases and it is free from any anxiety. Not only that, but it is also perfect in knowledge. In other words, it's not a blind type of bliss, but it is full of unlimited knowledge and consciousness. If I had that drink in a cup, and you knew that it was true, who would refuse it?

On the other hand, if I said to you that I have another drink in my other hand. This drink makes you temporary, so temporary that you can disappear and disintegrate. And this drink makes you full of misery and anxiety. It is a drink that will haunt you like a ghost. And not only that, as soon as you drink it your imminent death is certain. And to add insult to injury, it will taste horrible. Which one would you take?

Everyone can see this. And not only is this a fact here but it will be the same throughout the entire world. Why? Because it's explained that the Supreme Absolute Truth is *purnam*, complete. Krishna is completely perfect in every respect. He is also unlimitedly complete. In other words, we may have some completeness but in very limited quantities. If we're being honest, we could never say that anyone was perfect. We have not met anyone perfect. You could say, 'This guy is a genius in mathematics'. That could be said. But even then, it's a very limited thing because we know that actually knowledge is also unlimited, not just limited to mathematics. If you say you know everything in the universe, then I may say, 'Well, there are unlimited universes. Do you know everything in every single universe?' I don't think anyone's going to say that. Everyone must admit their incompleteness. But Krishna explains that the living entity is a fragmental portion of the arrangement that Krishna has designed. Krishna is a name for God. There is a complete arrangement in the human species, there is the highest manifestation of consciousness available.

We are very proud of our knowledge even though we cannot even see our eyelashes. Just to show you how limited we are, can anyone tell me how many eyelashes they have? Who can count? They are the nearest thing to your eyes. You're looking at them daily. If someone is thirty, that means for thirty years their eyelashes have been there right in front of them, and we have no clue how many are there. That shows that we are very limited. We are very proud that, 'Oh I can see into outer space', but we can't even see our eyelashes!

This is the difficulty with the fragmental living entity: he becomes very proud of his insignificant situation. Everybody is taking advantage of the sun, but what is the sun? Nobody knows. The scientists make a theory, 'Oh, it's some sort of gas or atomic combustion', or whatever. But actually, they have no clue. By limited perception, we cannot understand the unlimited. It is not possible. It's contradictory to think that you can understand an unlimited thing by limited perception.

The living entity must understand that he is limited in his sensory perception. His eyes are limited, they are also defective. Our vision is imperfect. Sometimes I see an object and mistake it for another. Every one of us tends to be under illusion. And we also commit mistakes. How many people can say, 'Oh, I've never committed a mistake'? Nobody - everybody commits mistakes.

Knowledge cannot be obtained simply by the limited mental speculation of the mind and intelligence. It can be obtained by going to a higher authority. If you want to understand any subject you must go to a higher authority. Sometimes when you are trying to catch a bus you go to the inspector, 'Can you tell me which bus goes to this destination?' You're accepting that man as an authority.

Throughout our life, we are always accepting authority. How many people sit down and watch the news on television and they say, 'Today in New York, there was a plane crash'. How many people believe it? Everyone does. But yet we see that all around there are different authorities. Every single one of us is accepting authority. You are all here tonight because you read some leaflet or got some information that something was happening.

The Vedas explain that if we want to understand the Absolute Truth that is beyond the limited perception of the mind and the senses, then we must approach the authority. Therefore Krishna says in the *Bhagavad-Gita*, 'Just try to learn the truth by approaching the bonafide guru, spiritual master. Inquire submissively from him and render service unto him. The self-realized soul can impart knowledge unto you because he has seen the truth'.

This knowledge comes down in the line of the *guru parampara* system or disciplic succession. Our *guru* has a *guru*, who has a *guru*, who has a *guru*, who has a *guru* - going back thousands of years. Therefore this knowledge is descending knowledge, not ascending. It is not that 'by my studying I will understand'. I must hear. It is descending from the transcendental realm. Therefore it is called revealed knowledge. Everybody takes shelter of some sort of knowledge such as in all of the scriptures we see throughout the world. Even if you want to be a materialist, you take shelter of mundane education and mundane knowledge. You go and get various types of qualifications. If you want to enjoy in the material world, then you become well equipped with knowledge. If you're ignorant, then you won't know anything.

Similarly, everybody is taking shelter of some type of knowledge. Material knowledge can only give us a very limited understanding and experience and it is also filled with the four defects - we tend to be cheated, to commit mistakes, to be under illusion and we have imperfect senses. What we're saying is that instead of taking shelter of temporary material knowledge, we should take shelter of that transcendental knowledge which can give direct spiritual perception of our real selves, to who we are, to where we're going, to why we're here. This knowledge can reveal to us the inner soul, the self.

It says in the Bhagavatam, *sai vai pumsam paro dharmo yato bhaktir adhoksaje, ahaituky apratihata yayatma suprasidati.* This knowledge gives the highest benediction to mankind. It is the supreme *dharma*. What is *dharma*? If you want to translate it into English, there's no equivalent, but it means the essential function of something. Just like the function of sugar is sweetness. And the function of salt is to be salty. So *dharma* is the innate function of the living entity, of the soul. This science of the Bhagavatam is the supreme *dharma* because it gives transcendental knowledge.

What is the supreme function of the self? The body is functioning. Where is the functioning coming from? It's coming from the soul. The soul is in the body and consciousness is manifested in the body. The body is functioning according to higher dictation. In society, you may say, 'I can do anything'. But then, when you drive your car, you have to stop at the red light. You may be Mr Rockefeller or you may be the Prime Minister of a country but you must stop at the red light. Does that mean that the red light is more powerful than the Prime Minister? That means the Prime Minister is a very insignificant thing because she has to also adhere to the law of the red light. So does that mean that the red light is a very powerful thing? No, it's not that. It's that the red light means higher authority. Every one of us has to be under the control of a higher authority.

The Vedas explain that each one of us is a tiny spiritual spark and its glory is in the relationship between the part and the whole. The whole means the complete Absolute Truth and the reservoir of all transcendental knowledge, bliss and eternity. This is what the word *yoga* means - the linking process between the small particle of spirit and God himself. That linking comes in this age through the process of chanting,

Hare Krishna Hare Krishna
Krishna Krishna Hare Hare
Hare Rama Hare Rama
Rama Rama Hare Hare

Chanting is given in this age as the most sublime method of linking the consciousness with the Supreme consciousness.

2: WHO IS THE DOER?

AT A PANDAVA SENA JAMMIN' YOUTH EVENT IN
EAST LONDON, UK - 3 NOVEMBER 2000

Bhagavad-gita 3.27

The bewildered spirit soul, under the influence of the three modes of material nature, thinks himself to be the doer of activities, which are in actuality carried out by nature.

When talking about the self, the natural inclination is to say that we are the body. There is an affiliation with the body due to our association with it. This association has to be studied very carefully as it is *asat*, a temporary relationship. As Krishna says that there is constant change, and the conditions of the body are transitory, changing constantly at every moment. New cells come in and old cells go out and there is a perpetual chemical interaction taking place. We find that the body and the mind are constantly changing. The mind in the morning is in one way and at noontime it's different and it's different a few hours later. If you think just for some time, you'll see that your mind has changed. The mind has no permanence. That is why you will find even in the sphere of education, you are constantly adding something. Why do you need to keep adding? Have you ever thought about that? You are always adding something throughout your life. Why? The reason is that we have a deficiency, an inadequacy - not only intellectually but also physically.

The body also needs constant support because it is a very delicate combination of different molecules and chemicals which need constant refurbishment or replenishment. If you don't eat or drink enough, you cannot survive. If you sleep too much or too little it also doesn't work. If you study it, you will find that you are constantly being forced into a situation of dependency. You cannot have either too much or too little. You have to find balance in the relationship between the body and nature. For balance, you need a certain amount of sleep. If you say, 'I will stop sleeping', or, 'I will stop eating', who can actually do it? Can you say, 'I will stop going to the toilet. I have decided I don't want to do these types of activities anymore'? Krishna explains in the *Bhagavad-gita* that the body is a machine. The psychological and physical functioning of the body is carried out by different forces of material nature or the different modes of nature. Krishna says, *prakrti kriyamanani,* all things are being carried out by material nature. Therefore, we have to understand nature itself. In the thirteenth chapter of the *Bhagavad-gita*, Arjuna asks Krishna about the relationship between matter (*prakrti*) and the individual soul (*purusa).*

What is your relationship with matter? You have a relationship with matter because you experience it. If you were experiencing something else, you'd have a relationship with that. The reason you have a relationship with matter is that you're experiencing matter. What type of experience is it? Is it a good experience or a bad experience? Or is it a mediocre experience? You have to understand that clearly. Your relationship with anything is through what? It's through experience. And experience comes through what? The senses.

According to the power of your senses, you have a certain type of relationship. That's what it's saying here, *prakrti kriyamanani,* according to your conditioned nature, you have a specific type of relationship. If you have a certain type of body, you have a certain type of relationship. Prabhupada said, 'You never see a crow becoming a swan'. If you put a crow in a beautiful lake, it will look for garbage. If you put a swan in a garbage heap, it will look for a lake. Everyone has association according to their body. The body is a product of matter on account of the relationship between the body and nature. The existence that you have in your body is according to your body's relationship with matter and according to your body's nature.

Sometimes you are happy because the conditions are better. You say, 'I'm happy today', 'It's sunny today. I've got money today. I've got love today'. Sometimes you say, 'I'm miserable today, I hate these people, I feel absolutely horrible!' These two types of experiences are what we call *sukha* (pleasure) *and dukha (*pain). When there is pleasure, we don't question our existence. When the experience is good we think that life is okay. We think that life is tolerable. 'Oh, it's quite nice. It's not so bad, don't be so pessimistic. Things will get better in the future. Things will improve. Technology is moving on now. They say they'll even get rid of wrinkles, old age and disease. After all, they did go to the moon, didn't they? So we should all be happy'.

We must understand the principle of faith because after all, knowledge is based on a certain amount of faith. Why do you think you're this body? Have you ever thought about that? There's nothing about this body that is attractive. If you put it all on a table - which you can do if you are in medical school - you take all the little bits and put them on the table and put little labels on them. Which of those bits are so good that you are willing to work your whole life to maintain them? Is it those little jiglets? Or is it the pumps? Or is it all those miles of veins that run around all over the place, or is it that mushy stuff called the brain? Which part is so wonderful, that you are totally obsessed with it and that it is very important for your happiness? This is called super-analysis of the human body. When you dissect your body even mentally, you'll find it's a combination of mechanisms. Your body has different types of systems, like the circulatory system or the digestive system. There are different types of mechanical systems operating. They are working very finely and very wonderfully.

When things are beyond our conception, we tend to have a certain amount of faith in them. Like faith in the body. Why do we have faith in the body? Because it's capable of giving you a superior experience. Although we give it a certain amount of superiority, the body itself is extremely inferior. It's not inferior because of its mechanisation, but because it does not exist permanently and the experiences through the body are very limited. And due to this limitation, they are incapable of satisfying the self. The reason no material experience satisfies the self is that the self isn't material.

You can give temporary satisfaction to the mind, depending on what you as the false ego feel that the mind should have. Some people get very excited about trainspotting. Others get very excited about collecting stamps. Some people get very excited about going out and meeting girls. Some get very excited about driving all sorts of cars and getting lots of money. Some people get excited about watching television. Some people get excited about being pretty and looking in the mirror all day. So these are all different types of stimuli to the mind. The stimulations of the mind are fleeting pleasures. You may have a good cigarette one minute but then a few minutes later you look for pleasure elsewhere. Prahlada Maharaja calls this principle, 'chewing of the chewed'.

Even though it gives pleasure, material pleasure is both limited and transitory by nature. It is happening in such a flickering way that you have to catch it again. You have to go looking for it again. If you notice, the nature of material pleasure is that you have to do the same thing over and over and over and over again. There is never a time when someone will say, 'I am now completely satisfied'. There's no experience in this world which satisfies the self. Some experiences give stimuli to the senses and mind. If you become intoxicated or engage in different types of stimulation, you'll find what it's doing to you is it's agitating you. There's a difference between satisfaction and agitation. Satisfaction means there's an awakening of something deeper than just the senses. Most of the experiences in the material world are a flickering reflection of real pleasure. They are not real pleasure. The experiences of the material world are a shadow of reality.

If you look at the experience of love in the material world, many of us have loved or been loved but you will find it fades after a period of time. Love itself exists under certain conditions. In the beautiful romances of marriage, when people get married they say, 'Oh, you are such a lovey dovey', and they love each other and cuddle each other and kiss each other. But gradually as time goes on, the kisses get less, the cuddling gets less and the relationship gets less. More and more contemptuousness comes in, and they get fed up with each other, sometimes to the point that they start hitting each other. It usually starts off with a bit of arguing, then you find that it deteriorates more.

That principle is described by Krishna in the *Bhagavad-gita* also, that in the beginning, when you have material pleasure in the mode of passion, it appears very sweet. That sweetness is there. The body is a good example of that. It starts off very sweet when it's young and vibrant. You have got this nice body and you're full of hope and aspirations, and gradually as this very amazing feature of time moves along, everything starts to become contemptuous. It starts to become disgusting. The very body you have becomes disgusting in old age.

As the body gradually progresses from youthhood to old age, we gradually feel our relationship with the body is becoming more and more dissatisfying. In the beginning, a material thing appears to be very sweet. But that sweetness gradually turns to poison. The pleasures of the material world will always end up in distress. I can guarantee that anything that begins pleasant, will end in distress. It doesn't matter what the reason is, but the very functioning of matter itself is to cheat the living entity.

The mind is the head of the senses. The mind through the agency of the senses is conducting this transitory relationship with the material world. And the soul stands convicted on account of our sinful activities in the material world. We are conducting our activities through the inferiority of this material body. Therefore, the activities themselves are inferior. You cannot get a superior result from an inferior instrument. What are you doing in medical science? You are always trying to get a better instrument. If you don't have a better instrument, you can't get a better result. Why are scientists always trying to come up with better instruments? To get a better experience. It's clear to us that the senses are totally inadequate. Life itself is a life of inexperience and inadequacy. Why? Because we have inadequate knowledge. The material world is perfect because it comes from the All-perfect. *'The Personality of Godhead is perfect and complete, and because He is completely perfect, all emanations from Him, such as this phenomenal world, are perfectly equipped as complete wholes. Whatever is produced of the complete whole is also complete in itself. Because He is the complete whole, even though so many complete units emanate from Him, He remains the complete balance'.* (Sri Isopanisad) Prabhupada explains in that purport that everything that comes from Krishna is perfect. But what I think is that everything that comes from this world contains imperfection. But Prabhupada said there is no imperfection, there is only imperfect knowledge of the complete arrangement of the complete. But everything is complete. This is actually very important - when we observe the universe, the planets, and how everything is functioning, we know that there's something superior going on. Prabhupada said, 'That is proof of God. God means superior'. When Prabhupada met Professor Kotovsky he said, 'You are accepting Lenin, and we are accepting Krishna. We are both accepting some authority. You may say your communism means disbelief in a God but Lenin is your God because you are accepting him as something superior'.

What is God? God is just something superior. How superior? Nobody knows how superior God is. We can say He is better than Lenin. Religion is just an acceptance of something superior, and everyone is accepting something superior. On account of our situation, we always have to surrender to something. Our instruments are defective, and due to that our knowledge is defective, therefore we must take shelter of something superior. If our knowledge was perfect, there would be no question of taking shelter in anything because we would not need to.

If our happiness was perfect, there would be no need to take shelter of anything. We wouldn't need to. Why do we take shelter in booze? Because we are unsatisfied. Why do we take shelter with women? Because we are unhappy. Why do we take shelter with different types of stimuli? Because we are unhappy. Everybody is taking shelter of something because of his inadequacy. We are dependent on that thing to give us some sort of superior experience. That superior experience is that thing we are hankering after. It is not the drink, not the women, not the booze, not the cinema, not Albert Schwarzenegger, but we want to see something superior. That's why most movies are about people doing superior things. A man beats up five hundred guys with one fist and everyone sits there saying, 'Wow!'

Everything we look at is on account of searching for something superior. We gravitate towards something superior. In actuality, when we talk about superiority, eventually it leads us to the realisation that we have to surrender. You have to take shelter of something for superior experience. Just like, we take shelter of our mind because it's superior to the dull senses. Krishna says in the *Bhagavad-gita* that the mind is higher than the senses. Why do you take shelter of your mind? You have a lot of confidence in your mind. Whenever you talk about engaging in activities, you'll have to bounce it off the mind. You have to make sure that anything you're going to accept or reject has to be passed through your mind. And then the mind will verify it with the other senses. Do you understand?

The senses are an extension of the mind. They verify by experience. We are totally and utterly dependent on the experiences of this world. But none of us can claim those experiences are adequate. We don't understand that there is a perfect arrangement in matter. Matter was created intentionally to give us an inferior experience. It's not coincidental that the experiences you get in this world are inadequate to your happiness. There is no one happy in this room. There is no one happy in this town. There is no one happy in this country. There is no one happy on this planet. There is nobody happy in the ocean or the sky. If you search through the trees and everywhere, you will not find one single creature that's happy. Isn't that amazing? If you study it further, you will find that every single animal, insect, bird, human, fish is looking for happiness, that's amazing. We are dealing with fundamental principles, that the principle of happiness is towards consciousness. And yet matter itself is incapable of giving any genuine experience of happiness. You cannot possibly say that is accidental. It doesn't make sense at all. It's natural to be happy and yet matter itself doesn't make you happy. Therefore, we have to bring in a higher factor.

Krishna explains, 'Knowledge of the field of activities and of the knower of activities is described by various sages in various Vedic writings. It is especially presented in Vedanta-sutra with all reasoning as to cause and effect.' (*Bhagavad-gita 13.5*) We are stuck in the effect, but we don't understand the cause. On account of our being too absorbed in that which is small, we have lost sight of that which is great. We don't understand that the cause and effect is coming from the superior, higher principle. Everything material needs coordination to bring about a superior thing. Your happiness absorbs you twenty-four hours a day. Why? Because it requires the full concentration of your mind and intelligence in order to bring about some organised form of activity. In any sphere, you need concentrated intelligence to bring about any organised form of existence. That is the difference between animals and humans. Humans are the only ones endowed with superior consciousness.

Animals do not organise themselves, but their activities are organised by nature. They are completely and utterly a manifestation of material conditions. The human being is the only one who can at least try to go above conditions. Why do we want to go above conditions? It is because the conditions themselves are not satisfying to us. They are not adequate. They are not substantial and therefore we are always trying to make adjustments. The human being is the greatest adjuster in this world. There is no one else who makes adjustments like the human being. The actual facilities of the material world are not better for humans than for animals. Prabhupada said that when an animal has sex, he has just the same experience as a human. It is not that you have such a superior experience. When an animal eats, he gets just as happy as you do. Some animals go into complete ecstasy when they eat. They are eating and they are sleeping. And they are just as attached to their family as you are. You think you're attached to your mum and dad, to your brothers and sisters, but they are just as attached. All of those things which you experience through the body, the animal is also experiencing through the body. The difference is that the animal cannot analyse his situation.

Human life begins with the power to analyse, which simply means that we have superior intelligence. Unless you have intelligence, you can't analyse. This analytical study of nature means that one can begin to understand the relationship between the five different elements of this world - the false ego, intelligence, the unmanifested, the ten senses and the mind, and the five sense objects. This interaction between senses and sense objects brings about what? Desire, hatred, happiness and distress - these are what are called the interactions which function within *bhoga* and *tyaga*, attraction and repulsion.

Within the scope of material experience, there is always some attraction and some repulsion. Once whilst Prabhupada was driving with some devotees, they saw a man get driven over by a lorry and the man was squashed all over the floor. Everyone was disgusted at the sight and turned to Prabhupada in shock. Prabhupada was just chanting on his beads and said, 'Why are you disgusted?'. 'Well Prabhupada, there was a man squashed on the floor, it looked horrible!' Prabhupada said, '...but you are the same!' So the thing becomes repulsive, although that very same thing is normally the most attractive thing in the world. People are dying for a woman or a man. The attraction between man and woman is so strong, but if you see a woman crushed by a thirty-tonne lorry on the M1 motorway it wouldn't stimulate you at all. As a matter of fact, you would probably run into the bushes and vomit. This is what we call *bhoga* and *tyaga,* desire and hatred, attraction and repulsion. Why is there a desire when the woman is nicely packaged and it's disgusting when it is splattered all over the floor? The same things are there, but it's not attractive to the mind. So the basic principle is that when we see a beautiful woman in a body, we have all sorts of hopes, aspirations, desires and dreams that we will be able to enjoy like this and that. Some nice *kiddie widdies* will come along with a nice house and wander around the garden. But then when they are squashed all over the floor, what do you do then? You can't say, 'Oh I'll put them together again! I will patch them all up! They do a lot of cosmetic surgery these days, I'll stick it all back in and repackage it all'.

The repulsion is because there is no more sense gratification. The principle of desire and hatred is based upon the principle of what you call 'anticipated psychology' or 'anticipation of happiness'. That, 'I will get my happiness from this thing'. Just like when you get your car, you feel great! 'I can do *this* now and *that* now'… suddenly, CRASH! You are crying, you are out there punching the guy because he didn't look where he was going and you are in total distress! You can't even talk to anyone for two weeks! You're in such distress! The same thing which was your object of pleasure, now becomes your object of distress, all because of a little change. The little change is that your sense gratification has been interrupted.

Krishna explains that from attachment comes lust. Lust is very important to study. This lust means the anticipated happiness that you're going to get something. 'From attachment comes lust and from lust comes frustration'. The whole material world is here to frustrate us. 'From frustration comes anger'. Have you ever noticed when you are trying to fix the smallest little thing and it doesn't work, you gradually end up smashing up the thing? You're shouting and screaming at it because it doesn't cooperate with you. Matter doesn't cooperate with you! That is the problem. Everybody needs to have cooperation for their own sense gratification. They need cooperation and matter does not cooperate with you. You cooperate with matter. That is the point of this verse. Material nature - *prakrti* is the doer. You are the co-operator. Therefore, in every situation, you are cooperating with the superior authority. All that Krishna consciousness says, is that you cooperate with the superior-most. That's all.

3: PROTECTING SOCIETY FROM IGNORANCE

A DEBATE AT UNIVERSITY COLLEGE DUBLIN
DUBLIN, IRELAND - NOVEMBER 1994

Professor: When you get transcendental trickery, check it out! All groups have a right to exist. Our friends from the Hare Krishna will be speaking next. Obviously, they're not brainwashing somebody because they're walking around telling you who they are. Other groups are walking around and not telling you who they are. And it's not necessarily the vulnerable people who join these movements, let me make that point. The people in the Solar temple included a Mayor, PhDs, very rich people; it isn't necessarily a bum on the street who joins a new religious movement. Anybody can join a new religious movement and it's anybody's right to do so but what I'm saying is before you believe - and that means spending rationality - check out, check out, check out. [Audience applause]

Our next speaker is a monk, Thomas from the Hare Krishnas. [Audience applause]

Tribhuvanatha: So many points have been raised and I'd like to also raise a few points of discussion. First of all, I'd like to say I'm not against the notion which has just been presented. I would definitely oppose certain aspects but then again, other aspects I wouldn't. The word 'religion' is also a very big word and it has different interpretations and meanings.

When you say orthodox religions, it's very hard to know what you mean by orthodox and unorthodox because if we say orthodox philosophy - religion is not orthodox philosophy. It's very unorthodox. As a matter of fact, most religions believe in things like raising the dead and the fact that God lives up in some dimension that we can't even approach, and the fact that we are going to have some sort of afterlife that we've never seen, and the fact that we believe in something which we have never had direct experience of. So what is orthodox? You might say something brought in the purview of our senses. Something which we can see, smell, taste, touch and hear. Is religion necessarily orthodox and is there such a thing as orthodox religion? I would
28

put the counter-notion, that there is no such thing as orthodox religion. There are conventional religions, religions which are to some degree or other bonafide, or not bonafide.

The Vedic literature explains that the actual purpose of life is to find out the truth. The concept of truth is something given very clearly in the Vedas, that it is the distinction between reality and illusion. The Vedas say that the whole purpose of human existence is to clearly understand the distinction between reality and illusion for the welfare of all. What we're saying is that education is supposed to be for the welfare and the benefit of the people.

Generally, what we find is that truth or knowledge brings a certain degree of mastership over matter. That's why in this university you have many materialistic sciences which you are all being educated in, to some degree or the other and then you are all accepting them as truth. Many of those sciences are based on theories and relative conceptions. Some of them are downright false. Some of those sciences which you call truth are as far from the truth as you can get. But that's a matter purely of opinion.

The real search for truth is to find out the cause of all causes because every single science is based on cause and effect. Some sciences posit that by studying the effect, you can understand the cause. In some sciences, by studying the effect, you get more confused about the cause. Religion is also one of those sciences which involve the study of cause and effect. You have what you call 'relative' and 'absolute' in philosophy. In material sciences, we're dealing with relativity and therefore we are dealing with people who are identifying with the body as the self and identifying with matter as being the main force in the universe. Therefore, their knowledge will always be relative to matter. But those who take to the spiritual path, they're looking for another goal which is to find out the absolute truth or God if you want to call it that. The problem with absolutism is its very unorthodox because we have no actual perception of anything absolute.

Absolute truths are called *axiomatic truths*; they stand the face of time. In other words, they are truths which always exist. Jesus Christ taught a message two thousand years ago, but it's still being studied in theological colleges throughout the world because Lord Jesus is teaching an absolute truth. If we want to protect people, the real education in society is we have to have an educational system which has its basis both on relative and absolute truth. If you want to protect people, the only way you can do that is by giving them knowledge. The difficulty you have is, as an example when you say 'dangerous cults', we would be branded amongst them to some degree or other, purely out of ignorance.

If you study Hinduism as an example, it's the third biggest religion in the world. The Hindu religion is very misunderstood because there's no such thing in the tradition as the word 'Hindu'. It doesn't exist. Hinduism is a group of philosophies based upon Vedantic literature, of which Buddhism is one offshoot, and it's an atheistic offshoot, but I won't go into that. The point is that there are two basic philosophies in Hinduism, the theistic and atheistic. The Hare Krishna is based on the theistic aspect of the philosophy, the devotional aspect, which is coming down in the last five thousand years.

I'd like to say that we have enough books on the philosophy that if anyone likes to read them, it could take you your whole lifetime to study. The problem is people are ignorant of the philosophy behind the Hare Krishna movement and therefore they tend to paint everyone with the same brush.

Professor: [Jokingly]: I'll just ask you, would that be the reason why you need reincarnation, so you would have time to read the rest of the books?

Tribhuvanatha: Yes! [Audience laughter] Very good point - you may have to come back to read the remainder. But one thing I would say is that an important point to understand is when you are throwing out the bathwater, don't throw the baby out as well. Do you understand?

There's a tendency to sort of paint everyone with the same brush. 'They're all dangerous, look at them, they've got shaven heads, and they wear bed-sheets. Oh my God! They should be strung up or kept away! They're a danger to our children! They're corrupting the very society that we live in! What I'd like to point out to you as an example, just with the Hare Krishna movement - we follow a tradition which has been passed down in India for thousands of years.

Many people would glorify a gentleman called Mahatma Gandhi - his whole philosophy was based on the same teachings of the *Bhagavad-gita* which we follow. We have principles: no meat-eating, completely adhering to non-violence; we don't even kill insects, unless they can kill you - that's the only exception. We don't take any kind of intoxication, no gambling and no illicit sex. We follow very strict rigid principles but at the same time, we are completely socially based. If I went to India dressed like this, I would practically get free travel on buses. Can you believe that? Just because I'm dressed like this. I could walk into the home of any man I want. And I've done this. Even politicians would never refuse me entrance into their home, all because I'm dressed like this. All because I follow the teachings of the Vedas. I've lived in India for five years, so I'm not speculating. If I go to colleges in India, I would be welcomed to speak to the students, on the philosophy of the Vedanta. But at the same time in another country, in another time, I could be crucified. I could be locked up - as we had in Russia - and be put through all sorts of brainwashing systems because of whatever cults are accused of.

I would not say that society should not be protected, but what I say is the first protection in society that should be given is against ignorance, and I think that is the main discussion here. I think the great lack in western society particularly, but also in eastern society now, is that we have pursued the philosophy of materialism which is, in reality, the religion of exploitation. We therefore have a big problem with the other philosophy - the philosophy of dedication. Religion is dedication. Materialism is exploitation.

I don't think therefore that we should then say that because our philosophy is based on exploitation and is very accessible and enjoyable, we should therefore immediately throw out anything which has any sort of dedication, which might require the adherents to get up early in the morning or chant various mantras from various books, or they might abstain themselves from different types of intoxications or meat or various things like that. The point I'm trying to make is that - yes, we should protect the students. Protect them with knowledge - and that is what you are being given and I think that unless you open up as universities and colleges and institutions of learning, unless you do open yourself up to studying various religions in-depth, then you will always have this ignorance which is causing destruction all over the world.

Why does a Protestant hate a Catholic? Because of ignorance. Christians go out and crucify and kill so many people in all the holy wars, generally because of ignorance. The same way the Muslims will go out and happily chop up a Hindu. It's all because of ignorance. It's not because they don't like the way they have their head shaved or the way that they wear bedsheets. It's because they don't know what the heck they're about. And just like any insect... I will give you one example, I'll finish on this. We see it many times, when people find an insect on the table…. BANG! [Slams the table loudly] It's dead. You know why? Because they didn't like the look of it. Thank you!

4: BODILY ATTACHMENT CAUSES DISTRESS

AN INTRODUCTORY LECTURE GIVEN
IN BIRMINGHAM, UK - 19 OCTOBER 1997

I'll give you homework, just like when you were at school. I want you to go home, chop off your hand and put it under a bus - you can put it in a paper bag if you want, so nobody sees it - let the bus run over it and you tell me whether you feel any pain or not.

So when the hand is connected to the body, it's very important and a lot of stress goes into it. You can do so many things with it when it is connected to the body. But when it is disconnected, you can't. Similarly, when your whole body is disconnected from your soul, you can put your whole body under the bus and you won't feel anything. Isn't that amazing? It's hard to believe that you could be underneath a fifteen-tonne bus and not feel anything. But it is a reality. If you're not in the body, how are you going to feel anything? It must be concluded that when you're inside the body, you're feeling things, but not that the body is feeling things. That's logical, isn't it?

Just like when you are inside your car, if someone hits it, you feel it. But if you're not in it, you don't feel anything. You come back and you find your car has been crushed, you feel it immediately and go into anxiety. Why don't you feel it personally? The reason is that you weren't in your car. But when you are in your car and someone hits your car, you become angry and you say, 'Why did you hit me you fool?' So many things happen.

It is the attachment to the car disturbing you, not the car. Some people are very wealthy and if their car was in a crash they'd say, 'It's insured don't worry!' Sometimes you crash into someone and they are glad you have crashed into them because they can claim it on the insurance. They say, 'Don't worry about it! Give it another bash, won't you? So that I can get some money on it!' They're quite happy for that to happen. I once saw a van flip over and crash into five other cars. One guy's car was crushed and he was in ecstasy, 'Oh great! I've got rid of it at last!' He could claim it on his insurance.

33

So it's relative. One man could come and say, 'Oh no, my car!', and become a nervous wreck and commit suicide. You don't know what he's going to do! But another man comes and is overjoyed. Why? Because the attachment is different, that is all. The same thing is happening but the mental attachment is different.

When we talk about the self, most people don't know what the self is, although they think they know. According to my mind, I am a body, I am English and I'm 40 years of age. I've got a job, a flat and a girlfriend. I've got so many thoughts in my mind telling me things. Those thoughts are not telling the dead body the same things. You find this in old age homes. You go to see them in the hospice and they tell you, 'I'm sorry he's gone'.
You say, 'Where has he gone? He's lying on the bed.'
'No, no, he has gone!'
It looks like he's on the bed, but he's not.
You could argue, 'No! Look! For goodness' sake! He's lying on the bed! I see his legs!' But the doctor says, 'No, he's passed away'.

So these are very important things to understand, otherwise, we are living in illusion. If we don't know who we are, how could we possibly make ourselves happy? If you say, 'I want to be happy', who is that 'I' that wants to be happy? If you say, 'I want to be perfect', what is that 'I'?

In the material world, people identify with the body as the self. They think, 'I am this body'. But that means you get old and you get diseased. That is your whole story in life. I can tell you what's going to happen to you in the future. I am a fortune-teller. You're going to get old, you're going to get diseased, and you are going to die. You can tell that to every single person on this planet. Whether it is a worm, a human, a goat or a chicken, you can go up to them and tell them about their futures. You don't need to be professional. You don't need to throw anything in the air or make any kind of cosmic arrangement. If a person takes on a body, then they're going to get old, they're going to get diseased, and they're going to die. We all do the same thing.

The only difference is that we have individuality and therefore think differently. That thinking process is very important. Our thinking is the beginning of our problem, not the body. Many people think the body is a problem. You may think, 'Well my body is causing me misery'. But the body doesn't really cause you misery. It is your attachment to the body that causes you misery.

Those who are attached to the body suffer and get pleasure. Krishna says, *matra sparsas tu kaunteya sitosna sukha dukha dah*, that there is a certain amount of pleasure and distress in this world. These are called relativities. We live in a relative environment. It's very important to study the word - *conditions*. When we say we are happy, it means that the conditions are making us happy. When it is sunny, one man feels happy, but another man feels miserable. If you're in Saudi Arabia and you say, 'It's sunny today', that doesn't mean you're going to be happy, because it is 128°F, but for another man living in Scotland, he may say, 'Today it's sunny', and he feels happy. So it is not the sunshine that is making him happy, it is the relative condition.

Another example is water. Sometimes if you jump into water it makes you very happy. Many people go to the Mediterranean Sea and jump in the water, and they feel very happy. But at the same time, if you jump in freezing cold water, you won't feel happy. Does that mean that the water is causing misery or does it mean that the water is causing you pleasure? The water doesn't cause pleasure or pain. Water is water. What is causing happiness and pain is how you relate to the water. What is your relationship with the water? If you are in the middle of winter and you jump in the water you are not going to have a good relationship with the water. You are going to freeze, so you become unhappy. The important thing is our relationship with that thing. The thing itself is not the problem, it's our relationship. The body is not the cause of our suffering, it is our relationship with the body.

Many people become disturbed when they get older and their hair starts to fall out. It is not a good thing when you comb your hair and suddenly half of it falls out, or if your teeth fall out at breakfast. You are having your cornflakes and you find your teeth in your cornflakes. To some people, that would be very disturbing, because they will start to think, 'Oh what is going on here?' The body is starting to disintegrate.

This happens with anything material, it doesn't matter what it is. You can pick the most beautiful rose, it will only last a certain time and then you throw it away because it starts to bug you. The same rose that you gave to your loved one starts to look like a shrivelled up old flower. A boy gives a girl a beautiful rose and she gets very excited. But that same rose when it becomes withered becomes disturbing to the mind. The natural inclination of consciousness is that we are attracted to certain conditions. Krishna says that we are attracted to certain conditions and we are repulsed by other conditions.

We love our body. It is the best thing that we've got. We think we aren't going to get any better. It could get worse but it's not going to get much better. We can put on all sorts of odour and cologne and makeup and all sorts of funny things to make it look a bit better. We can get a bit stretched here and a bit stretched there but the point is things are not going to get much better. We are very attached to our body but the attachment isn't to the body, but the specific condition of the body. We want it to be in a very good condition but unfortunately, the body itself is influenced by circumstances beyond our control.

The important thing is control. Who is in control of this thing? Just like if you are in a car going down the motorway at a hundred miles per hour, it can be great right? You are enjoying yourself, listening to your stereo playing music, but if your driver is suddenly falling asleep on you and the car is swerving this way and that way and he's insisting, 'No, no it's all right! Don't worry!' You are in anxiety. The same thing that was giving you pleasure now is giving you tremendous anxiety. Nobody goes looking for distress. Nobody wants to get stressed or anxious. Anxiety is when our mind is disturbed. This stress comes whether we want it or not.

Even if you decide, 'I'm just going to sit in my room and I'm not going to go out because when I go out I get in distress', you still get distressed even when you just sit somewhere because suddenly your mind starts causing you distress. It starts saying, 'What are you doing here?'
And you reply, 'I'm sitting here'.
The mind says, 'What are you doing, you shouldn't be sitting here'.
You reply, 'No, no, I want to sit here'.
'I know, but you should be enjoying yourself!'
'Really?'
And then the mind says, 'You should be enjoying yourself! You should be happy! You're as miserable as sin. You are a miserable and rotten person!'
So that reminds you, 'Oh yes, I should be happy. I should mix with people'.
As soon as you start to sit in that place you get into these mental anxieties.

In actuality, whether you are inside, outside, upside, downside, you are going to be in anxiety because the material world is called *kuntha*, that place which gives you anxiety. The conditions of this world are created to give you anxiety. The person controlling these conditions is called God. God created the material creation for a specific purpose. It didn't just happen accidentally as people like to think. Behind every activity, there is an intelligent design. There is an arrangement behind this universe. There is an unlimitedly powerful design, the desire of God. Just like you and me - He has a personality. He is a person, and He is a designer. We also design things. We design things because God designs things. In the Bible, it says God created man in his own liking and to his own image.

The difference is that our designs are very tiny. We design a car or an aeroplane, but this planet is like a big aeroplane floating in space. In two and a half billion years it hasn't crashed yet. If you could have an aircraft in the air for two and a half billion years and it doesn't crash, that's a pretty good safety record. The universal order is so wonderfully created by God. He doesn't create crashes. We are the ones that are on this planet doing all the crashing and criticizing Him for making mistakes.

We're the ones that have messed up the atmosphere.
We're the ones that have messed up the water system.
We're the ones that have messed up our lives.
We're the ones that messed up the countryside.
We're the ones that have messed up the education of our children.
We're the ones that have messed up our relationships with each other.
We're the ones that have messed up our political systems.
We're the ones that are fighting with each other, killing each other, murdering each other, raping each other, stealing from each other and we're all blaming God. We are all sitting here saying, 'Look what a mess You have made of this place!'

This is our consciousness – because we're cheaters. The material energy is created under specific laws and it works without one single microscopic movement beyond what God wants. Some people will turn around and say, 'Well, why do bad things happen then?' That's always the anti-Christian argument. Or another argument, 'If God is so great, why does He let that happen?'

The point to understand is that as an individual entity, we have unique individual independence and according to Vedic knowledge the living entity comes to the material world to exercise his independence under certain laws. We are infinitesimal and we are a tiny particle of God, therefore we have an infinitesimal capacity. It's like one ray of sunshine has the quality of the sunshine but if there is a little molecule of the sun in your room you can't say the sun planet is in your room. Similarly, we are a tiny fragment of God, therefore, we have the qualities of God in a very fragmental, tiny proportion. In the material world, we are acting according to certain desires. Everyone has a desire. That desire is called separatism. We are separatists. Separatist means we have a separate interest from God. Spiritual life means to have no separate interest from God.

If you want to know why you're suffering in this world, it's because you have a separate interest from God. Who is a good example of someone who's supposedly suffered, but actually didn't suffer? In the Christian religion, it's Jesus Christ. He was crucified on the cross but three days later he was walking around because he had no separate interest. Those who have the same interest as God are not controlled by material laws. The living entity, the soul himself, does not belong in the separatist environment. Krishna says in the *Bhagavad-gita*, 'This material energy is my separated energy consisting of earth, water, fire, air, ether, mind, intelligence and false ego'.

The soul has nothing to do with these energies. The soul belongs in the spiritual world with God but because he has forgotten that eternal relationship with God, he's living in ignorance. Krishna consciousness means to wake up! Wake up the consciousness to understand that this entire cosmic universe is God's His sporting ground. Sporting means you do something because it is there to give you pleasure. God enjoys creating the universe. He created it in his form of Vishnu.

Why does God enjoy creating a horrible place? That is a common question. It is because He desires to fulfil the desires of every entity. We are part and parcel of God. So for us to pursue our independence of God, He gives us a particular type of body. Just like if you have a son or daughter, they may want to do things that you don't want them to do. Many parents experience that when their children grow up. They want to go here and there and listen to a certain type of music and hang out with a certain type of people. They have a different philosophy and a different value system. So what does the father do? He has to accommodate the child. Even though he may not agree, because there's a relationship with the child, the father allows the child to have some freedom. Sometimes the child wants to go to the disco, the father and mother say, 'No, it's not good to go to these discos, you might meet this guy, this might happen, that might happen', but at the end of the day, most parents end up giving the children money to go to the disco, even if they don't want them to do it, due to affection. Similarly, the living entity wants to enjoy independently of Krishna and Krishna has affection. 'Man proposes and God disposes'. Krishna creates the facilities.

There are a lot of people on this planet who say, 'I'm having a great time, I don't give a hoot about whether God exists or not. It doesn't mean anything. I have good money. I have good facilities and I have got enjoyment. I don't need your love. If you have a problem and you need money, fine, but I'm having a tremendous time. I think this world is wonderful'. It's not that everyone is suffering. There are lots of people who consider that they are having a great time but when people suffer, that's when they blame God. You never see anyone writing an article, 'Oh my God! Look what God did - I won the lottery last week! Why should He go and do that? I have now got the burden of winning 16 million pounds!'

Why do people only complain to God when things go wrong? When things are going good, nobody thinks about God. And when things go wrong that is when He blew it, that's when He made all the mistakes. That is when He did his homework wrong. That's when He got his arithmetic wrong. God did everything wrong. When things don't go the way you want, then He's a big bad guy and He should be sacked. Or sometimes they say He's dead or senile or an old cripple in the hills. But when everything is going right, there's no mention of God.

People don't remember God when they are enjoying themselves. It's only when there is suffering. And that is why suffering exists. It's there to remind us, to awaken us to remember we don't belong in this environment. This is not our environment! Why? Because it's inferior. Anything separate from God is inferior. Of course, on a higher level, there is no separation from God as He creates everything so it's all His energy, but this energy is created in the mode of ignorance and when there is ignorance about God, there is misery.

If you take a five-year-old child from its mother and put it in the Hilton hotel and give it all sorts of wonderful facilities the child would cry its eyes out because the separation from the mother is intolerable. It doesn't matter what you give the child. It will not be happy because the child cannot be happy without the mother. Similarly, the living entity cannot be happy without God. It is not possible. He may entertain himself for a while. He may run around for a while, hopping around thinking he's getting somewhere or he may have so many Illusions, but in actuality, he can never be happy.

The misery of the material world is the mercy of God. It is a concession of God because He's showing us, 'You don't belong here you fool! Wake up and understand this is not your real position!' Old age is the kindness of God. When you get old you begin to awaken. If you see any church in this country, I will guarantee you ninety-five per cent of the congregation are people over the age of fifty. You go to any Hindu temple and you will find most of the congregation is at least over the age of forty. You go to any synagogue, it's the same thing. At the same time if you go to any night club or disco you'll only find young people and you won't find anyone talking about God.

If we all remained young, we would all still be bopping around in discos for millions of lifetimes. So, therefore, it's the kindness of Krishna, that He shows us that when we are ready to go to the disco, 'Ouch my back hurts', 'Oh, I'm getting too old for this'. Have you ever heard the phrase, 'I'm getting too old for this?' Krishna out of His kindness is telling you, 'Hey listen! It's time to get serious! This old bag of bones that you have been dragging around all of your life is starting to deteriorate!' And that is why there are so many hospitals. Wherever you go there is always a big hospital with lots of people moaning, 'Oh my head! My arm! My back!', because in actuality Krishna is telling them, 'Listen, you don't want to come back here again! Finish your business in this life, don't waste another lifetime!'

That's why the material world is created so wonderfully. It provides a certain amount of pleasure and it provides a certain amount of pain, and in between, you have to make decisions. Your position is, you can either say, 'Okay, I want to stick it out here and fight to the death and see if I'm going to be happy' or if you are intelligent you can say, 'I have done this thing long enough. I have smoked cigarettes before. I have had this before. I have had that before. I have chased after the opposite sex. I have watched thousands of videos and films, and read the newspapers until they fall out of my hand. I want to start looking for something more'.

Spiritual life means becoming greedy for knowledge. In the material world, people become greedy but what is their greediness? Their greediness is that they want more suffering because if you become more attached to the body then all it means is that you're going to be born, get old, get diseased and die. Becoming greedy in spiritual life means to be eager to realize that I want to find out about myself. I want to know who I am, what I am, where am I from, where am I going and who is controlling me?
That is the beginning of spiritual life, *athato brahma jijnasa:* now is the time to wake up. Stop sleeping in the material world, constantly dreaming about that one day that it's going to get better - because I can tell you, getting old, diseased and dying does not mean it's getting better. The whole incompleteness in the material world is not incomplete at all but it's a complete arrangement so that you can understand actually I have to stop this silly business of trying to enjoy that which is not enjoyable and begin my real business which is service to Krishna.

We have been dedicated to this body. We have done wonderful things and miserable things for the body but at the same time, the body itself does not show appreciation because the only thing that your body does after you have spent eighty, ninety or a hundred years cleaning it, looking after it, serving it, bringing it nice foodstuffs, all that it does is it just it falls down, *plomp*, dead. That's its thankfulness. After all of that work you did, it just goes *boom* and that's not very grateful, is it? After a hundred years of service. In reality, it is like a man who builds a big house, spends millions of pounds and years and years of his time and then the whole house collapses. How would he feel?

Suppose you spend a hundred years building a house, putting nice things in it, decorating it, looking after it and then the whole thing just goes *pshew* like a pack of cards. You would feel pretty fed up, wouldn't you?

At the end of your whole lifetime of serving the body, getting things for it, making sure it's in a nice warm bed, making sure it has a nice bath, making sure it has nice varieties of toothpaste to use, making sure it has got nice facilities and a car to sit in and all the rest of it - all it does is keel over. And then when it falls over after all that work, they come and put it in the dustbin. They pick it up, 'Oh no get it out of here! Quick! Get him out of here! He's causing a nuisance here!' Suppose you were found dead in the middle of Birmingham High Street, what would they do? 'Oh no! Get him out of here!' They would bring an ambulance. And then when the ambulance gets the body, they immediately want to stick it in the ground very quickly. Everyone is trying to get rid of it.

After all of that work that you put into the body - society and everyone else is trying to get rid of it and if they can't get it into the ground, they stick it into a fire, or they start chopping you up and using you for experiments or other things. At the end, no one is very grateful for all the service you did. The only response society has is they throw you away. So when you die you leave a little note saying, 'Listen, I have worked hard on this body! Give it a little respect'. That's what people do. They give you a little bit of respect. They take you in a nice car on the way to the crematorium. The reality of it all is that you are an insignificant product of matter that was flapping around for a few years and then you disappear. You are put back into the energy again. The earth goes back into the earth. The water goes back into the water. The fire goes back into the fire, ether goes back into the ether, and the mind travels off on its journey into a new body, carrying with it all of the misconceptions it collected. This is called 'false ego'. The special benefit of the human body compared to other species is that it's for spiritual life. Finishing up with this changing bodies program. I'm going back home.

5: YOU CANNOT TELL GOD WHAT TO DO

EXCERPTS FROM A TALK GIVEN AT MAKERERE UNIVERSITY
KAMPALA, UGANDA - OCTOBER 1996

Tribhuvanatha and his team held an event with 500 students at Makerere University, the most prominent University of Uganda, based in the capital city of Kampala. Many people who attended the event were challenging him on stage.

Tribhuvanatha: Every one of you, you say, 'My body'. But where are you inside the body? Come on point! Are you in here? Suppose you say, 'I'm in here' [pointing to the head] and we take your head and pull out the brain, is that you? Suppose we put it on the table, is that you on the table? Suppose you say, 'I'm in here' [pointing to the heart] and we take out your heart or your chest and put it on the table. Is that you on the table?

Lady in audience: Our God sent His son Jesus! We follow Jesus because there is no other way! Hare Krishna is from the devil!

Tribhuvanatha: Well, the thing is people don't have a very broad mind, they are very narrow-minded. They think that, 'My religion is the best, and that other person I should kill him!' They think, 'I should kill him because he's not like me'. Just like many people have come to your country and because you didn't like them - they killed you! This is called sectarianism. It's called prejudice. It's called something which is very narrow-minded; because actually, all of us are sons of God. We are all sons of God, whether we're African, Chinese, English or Irish; whether we are Christians, Muslims, Jews, we are all sons of God...
The difference between the material world and the spiritual world is that the material world is limited whereas the spiritual world is unlimited.

Lady in audience: ...and Jesus is the only link!

Tribhuvanatha: Those people who think that God is only for them are very limited because God is available to everyone! God is available to everyone!

Do you think that God is so limited, that he can't be available to everyone? He *is* available to everyone! He's not so small-minded.

I'll give you an example: money is available in every country, not just in Africa. Suppose I come to your country and I say, 'Oh we only have money in England, in other countries they don't have money', that's a stupid thing to say, isn't it? Similarly, if you say God is only available in your religion and not in others that is a stupid thing to say! [Audience applause] And there are billions of dead people in coffins because of that statement!

Yes, because of that statement, because of that narrow attitude millions of people have been killed in the history of the world because someone is thinking, 'My country is the best, therefore, let me go and kill this other country!' or 'I am better than you, therefore, let me subject you', or 'My religion is the best and yours is not so good'. This is what we call religious arrogance. You are dependent. Everyone in this world is born into dependency, but God is independent! He is independent! And if He wants, He can send 100 billion representatives! It's His choice! You cannot tell God what to do and what not to do.

Man in audience: Why don't Hare Krishna people eat meat?

Tribhuvanatha: We believe that all animals are also part of God and they have a right to life. So we don't eat any meat. We don't slaughter animals. We don't cut the throats of innocent cows! Because it also says in our friend's teachings, 'Thou shalt not kill'. Killing is actually evil. If you commit violence - violence will come after you! That is called the 'Law of *karma*'. Did you know that? For every action you do, you will get a reaction. 'As you sow so you shall reap'. Whatever action you do in this world has a subsequent reaction. Many people think that, 'I will go to Church and worship God', but then afterwards they will eat the chicken.

If you like to eat meat, why don't you go out into the jungle and eat the lions? They're also very tasty. The reason you don't eat the lions is that they may eat you! This is called violence! You are committing violence upon those who can't defend themselves, therefore this is called bullying! You are a bully!

Man in audience: Krishna is dead! Jesus is the living God.

Tribhuvanatha: These are what you call uneducated statements. They are uneducated statements. If someone reads our books, we will be happy to discuss with them who Krishna is and whether He's alive or dead! If you go out into the desert and you meet someone who has been in the desert all of his life and he comes up to you and says, 'Oh, your mother is dead!' How does he know whether she's dead? He doesn't even know your mother. It's not even an intelligent question to ask because Krishna is not dead. Krishna is not a material body. He is not made of matter. The word Krishna simply means all-attractive. Allah means the Almighty. Jehovah means the all-powerful.

The attractiveness of God is the most important feature of God. If God is not attractive then there is no meaning to God because that means you will be attracted to something else, isn't it? Suppose you say that bananas are more attractive than God - that means a banana is greater than God! So if you don't know what God looks like - how will you know whether He's attractive or not? It's a fair comment, isn't it? Suppose I said to you, our wonderful Christian brethren, can you describe the face of God? What does He look like? Answer! [Audience applause] And... I will request you one thing, don't tell me He looks like Jesus Christ because Jesus Christ said, 'There is one greater than me, my Father, It's Him whom you worship!' 'My Father is the one you worship'. [Audience applause]
So you tell me about the face of your Father!
What is the face of the Father? What does He look like?

6: THE PSYCHOLOGY OF AFFECTION

Everyone in the material world is born into delusion. We have deluded consciousness. It is compared to when you pollute water: water is pure but it becomes polluted when it is mixed with mud. So in the same way, we have polluted consciousness. The delusion of the material world is based on affection or *sneha*. This is a very important aspect of life. Everybody has some affection for something and that affection is affecting us. Everyone has affection for his body. We are madly in love with our body. We think that there is nothing better in the three worlds than us. That is the reason we don't like to be embarrassed. We like to hide behind the saying, 'Well, I may not be perfect, but I am close enough'. In the relative world, the living entity's affection is that he wants to be independent of Krishna. We have an affection that we want to be separate from Krishna. Everyone is very much under the control of this *ahankara* - this false ego of the mind. We create many different types of illusions. This affection is on account of that association. If you go into a room full of beautiful women, you will feel affection. If you're in a room full of ugly women, the affection will be less. If you go to a geriatric unit in a hospital, you're not going to get too excited. But if you go to a nice beauty contest with lovely-looking, shaking girls, the mind will become excited.

This psychology of affection is very important as it can reveal so many things about the nature of the mind. The mind naturally is attracted or repulsed to sense objects. If we study the nature of attraction it is always based upon the idea of sense gratification. We want to bring in something very nice for our senses to enjoy. So we're always hungry after that thing. Christmas time is a very good time. People are very busy but the same objective is there, to get something nice. In America, there's one toy that if you tickle its tummy it laughs, and if you tickle it again it laughs even more and if you tickle it the third time, it goes completely berserk. People are willing to spend five hundred dollars for that toy, even though it costs like twenty-eight dollars to manufacture. People are willing to pay an enormous amount for it because their kids have some affection for it. Their idea is that if you buy the children a nice toy, they'll be happy. But after a week or two, the kid completely loses interest in it. These are stupid parents. One parent flew from America to England to buy this toy and bring it back. This is how crazy these people are.

In the material world, so many things are objects of our affection. The human being is much more developed in consciousness. An animal has affection for the grass but we want to taste nicer things. If I showed you a nice double cream vegetable *sabji*, your mind would be shaking and your whole equilibrium is disturbed, 'Oh, how can I get my teeth into that?'

We are kept in the material world due to the nature of the tongue. If you look at all of the animals, practically speaking their whole concentration goes down through the tongue. You may see a big tiger or a lion, as soon as you throw it food, their whole concentration and their whole affection moves. Some animals will even fight with their children or wife. They'll bite them. They'll bite anything that comes.

The nature of the tongue is to vibrate and to taste. These two things are very attractive to the tongue. We want to vibrate our tongue to communicate the wonderful reservoir of knowledge within our mind. We are so puffed up with the empty space between our ears. We think there's so much there that we can communicate to the world, as if the whole world has been waiting for us to come and reveal to all of them the wonderful speculations that have been going on in our mind since time immemorial. Everybody wants to vibrate their tongue, even if they've got nothing to talk about. Every pauper is proud of his miserable old penny. We think we have something important to give and that gives us some sort of self-importance. That we are worth something, but man is worth what he speaks. Practically speaking a fool can be immediately known if he opens his mouth. You can immediately suss this person out, 'This guy is an idiot, a thickhead, a dumbnut' – or 'This man is very intelligent. This man is very advanced in knowledge'. What is the nature of these sound vibrations? Simply talking about all of the different illusionary things we see.

This material world is known as the ocean of names. Everything has a particular name. It is very important to study this psychology of names. Names are meaningless, but they give an indication to something. They don't give the fact of something. For instance, by saying the word gravity we appear to have grasped the concept, but actually, it's cheating to say the word gravity, because we don't even really know what gravity is. We know what the word is, but we don't know what it is referring to. You might say, 'It's the law of gravitation', or, 'something floats under that law', but in actuality, none of us understands gravity. We say the word 'sun', but nobody understands the sun. But because we have given it a designation, it has come into our expecting jurisdiction. We have brought it into our jurisdiction. We have named it, departmentalised it and put it under our control. This is the nature of the material world. We like to put everything within a name. As soon as a new thing comes out, it's immediately entered into the dictionary. Now they're even inventing slang words, so everything can be named very nicely. But in actuality, nothing is understood about the thing. If I say my name is 'John Smith'. What does 'John Smith' mean? Does it have any actual meaning of who I am?

In spiritual life, we say that Krishna means all-attractive and Rama means the reservoir of all pleasure. They have meaning. But within the material world, all of these various types of names are meaningless. They are all the inter-reactions between the senses and sense objects. In one country they have a name for something and in another country, it has a different name. But still, the point is that all of these things are simple manifestations of the three modes of material nature. By themselves, they have no actual spiritual meaning. Materially they might have some connection.

The tongue is very powerful because it likes to enjoy foodstuffs, it likes to drink intoxicating liquor. It likes to take all sorts of nice foodstuffs, juicy, tasty, succulent things. In that way, the tongue keeps us very much bound by affection to the material world. That's why in the *yoga* systems it's very important not to cater to the tongue. Because the whole understanding of the system of *yoga* is the more you cater for your senses, the more you become subject to the objects of the senses. The more you become an actual servant of the objects. The more you serve your senses, the more faithful you become to the objects of the senses. You become subservient to those objects.

I have a wife, she's very beautiful, and so I serve her very nicely. She serves me and I become very attached because she serves me very nicely. She gives me a little peck on the neck before I go out. And she has a nice sweet-smelling body. It actually smells diabolical but they put some perfume on to cover it. This is affection. And she calls me sweetie pie. So my heart is going *boom, boom, boom.*

Why? Because most people are just looking for affection. They need affection. The soul is very affectionate. Krishna is the reservoir of all affection. He is the reservoir of all personality. He is the Supreme Personality. The natural affection of the living entity is meant for Krishna. The spark of the fire, although minuscule, has the same quality as fire. The fire has the ability to burn, it has heat, light, and energy. Similarly, by studying one little drop of water, it can give you the constitution of water. In the same way, the constitution of the soul is affection. But that affection is misdirected in the material world on account of association.

One time on a morning walk with Prabhupada, there was some ice on the ground and he was hitting it with his stick and asked, 'What is this?' Someone said, 'Prabhupada, that is ice'.
Prabhupada said, 'No, that is originally water, but in association with the cold it has become hardened, it has become rock hard'.

If you throw some water on someone, it's not so bad, but if you throw a lump of ice on them you can cause some serious injury. So because the living entity is separated from Krishna in the material world, his heart has become very hard. What is that hard-heartedness? That hard-heartedness is on account of association with *kama*, lusty activities. These lusty activities make us very, very, demonic. Demonic means hard-hearted. Anyone can understand that. Crooks, robbers and thieves are all very hard-hearted people. They'll go and shoot someone in the head and take their money or rape an innocent woman or murder some child.

The real meaning of consciousness is lost on association with matter. The original nature of the consciousness of the living entity is love and affection. They are inseparable. When one has love, then automatically one has affection. This nature of love is covered over in the material world. The living entity very much suffers on account of these false attachments. The nature of *maya* is that if you become attached to something, proportionate to the amount of attachment you have for that thing, to that degree you will suffer. To the degree that you are attached - to that degree, you will suffer. Anything in this material world will only bring you suffering. It brings you suffering because it's temporary.

A man is very much in love with his child. He loves his beautiful little twelve-year-old daughter. She kisses him, she loves him... and then suddenly she's dead! And the man is broken-hearted. The whole world becomes vacant. The whole universe becomes vacant. And we see so many times when a boy loves a girl very intensely and then she dies in a car crash or something, then he also commits suicide. He left a little note saying, 'Julie, I couldn't live without you, my heart was broken! My heart was so broken. I was going crazy all day and night!' So the pain of jumping off of a fifteen storey building is nothing compared to the pain of missing Juliette in this world. He was so much broken-hearted for Julie. His heart was broken in a million pieces. Somebody else is crying, 'I never got over it when mum died. I never got over it, my heart was broken!'

In that way, we become broken-hearted. This breaking of the heart is *maya's* business. *Maya* is there to break your heart! There's another word for *maya* that means, 'One who makes you cry forever', 'One who makes you cry eternally'. *Maya* will make you cry and cry. 'I wanted that thing! But it didn't stay for very long!' That is the nature of this material world. We are very eager for that thing. We are very lusty after that thing, but unfortunately, that thing will not stick around. It will not stay. Even this body won't stay. I love my body so much, my body is so dear to me, I'm thinking about it twenty-four hours a day and in front of my very eyes, it is disintegrating. It's falling apart. This is the nature of the material world. Everything that you put your affection into gets lost. The nature of material nature is to kick you. *Maya's* business is to kick you. *Adhyatmika*. Miseries of the mind. We are very attached to our mind even though it has caused us unlimited misery.

Still, we think,
'I think the problem is...',
'I think the actual situation is...',
'I think that person doesn't understand me',
'I think I'm a really nice guy! But nobody understands how nice I am',
'I think this is a real problem',
'I think these guys are all a bunch of demons'.

This is the nature of I, me and mine. The word 'I' is very demonic. As soon as you say, 'I' you are a *maha raksasa*, big demon. Prabhupada always used the word 'we'. Did you notice that? Bhaktisiddhanta Sarasvati Thakura also always used 'we', because the living entity is never 'I' in the material sense. 'I' means separated consciousness. 'We' means 'Krishna and I'. That is the real point.

In the Srimad Bhagavatam, we see many examples of people being affected with affection to something. Particularly Arjuna and Yudhisthira Maharaja. As soon as they showed some affection, immediately their whole mind was completely disturbed. Yudhisthira Maharaja was completely disturbed because so many people died on the battlefield of Kuruksetra. He was the son of Dharmaraja (the lord of *dharma*, religious duty) and he was feeling great affection, 'Because of me, all of these people suffered and died from these wounds!' How many millions must have been marriage-less, husband-less, son-less? Even Arjuna lost his son. They were all son-less. They were all suffering and crying. There was tremendous suffering. Yudhisthira Maharaja couldn't tolerate it. 'Oh Krishna, what have I done? I have caused so much pain! Just so that I could be reinstated as King'. Even though Krishna tried to explain to Yudhisthira Maharaja that this was all providence, it was predestined by the nature of *kala*, time. Krishna says, 'Time I am and I have come to destroy all of these soldiers'. Krishna had come as time.

The business of time is to destroy. So why should we be worried if something's destroyed? That's the business of time. It's like crying because water is wet. It's the nature of water to be wet. You can't jump in the water and hope to get dry, can you? That's a ludicrous proposition. So you can't live within the ocean of time and not expect to get things destroyed. It's a ludicrous proposition because time destroys everything. We have practical history.
Every empire that has come has been destroyed.
Every business that has come has been destroyed.
Every man that has set foot in this world has been destroyed.
Every animal that has set foot in this world has been destroyed.
Every bird that has flown in this world has been destroyed.
Every fish within the ocean has been destroyed.

We should be amazed if anything isn't destroyed! That should be our amazement. But the fact that something is destroyed is very natural, so why should an enlightened person lament? Krishna says, 'He who is wise laments neither for the living nor for the dead'. If we are actually wise, there's no need to lament. It's a fact of life that we are going to be destroyed.

The country that we are in is going to be destroyed.
The planet we are situated on is going to be destroyed.
The sun shining on our heads is going to be destroyed.

The universe is going to be destroyed.
The whole billions of universes are going to be destroyed.

Destruction is the very nature of matter, time. It is not behoving of Yudhisthira Maharaja to lament because this was predestined. And Yudhisthira Maharaja was also destroyed. We are reading about Yudhisthira Maharaja because he's not around anymore, so it's a practical example. He was lamenting for them but later on he also went. We are here lamenting and lamenting, but we will also be gone. It is just a phantasmagoria. We are trying to build a castle in the sky. We should not lament for anything in this world, no matter what happens. It is all the inter-reaction between the senses and the sense objects.
Therefore, Lord Caitanya says, 'Unfortunate as I am I have no attraction to You'. That is the real lamentation. This is called *vipralambha*. *Vipralambha* means when we are very much disturbed and upset, feeling the separation of Krishna. Why am I not with Krishna? Why am I still attached to this miserable bag of skin and bones and stool and urine and pus and different types of tubes and pipes? Why am I still affected by all this garbage, mucus and bile? Because affection is still there. We should not lament for such things. We are lamenting for a bag running around made of skin, bones, stool and all these tubes.

Krishna consciousness is a scientific analysis of the material world and the situation of the living entity. All of the inter-reactions: *kama* (lust), *krodha* (anger), *lobha* (greed), *moha* (illusion) - these things have to be understood, so as to get out of this pitiful situation. Sometimes these great devotees come to show us by example what a pathetic situation we are in. Krishna says, *matra sparsas tu kaunteya sitosna sukha dukha dah*, we should learn to tolerate. Sometimes we feel very happy and at other times we are so absolutely stinking miserable that we can't even look at each other. Because we are absorbed in our mind. We have taken affection for the mind. We have taken affection for the genitals, the tongue, the belly and all of the senses. We want that thing over there. We are going mad for those objects. We are dreaming day and night. As soon as you see a beautiful girl, affection immediately comes pounding on the heart, 'Let me embrace her, let me have some relationship with her'. So this is m*aya*, delusion, one who is deluded by the false concept of existence.

Devotee: Sometimes it's very bewildering how people continue the illusion of material life, despite knowing all of these facts...

Tribhuvanatha: Yes, it's because until they're instructed properly, there's no alternative. If you're ignorant of something, then you're like a frog in a well. Until something assists you from outside, you're just simply wandering around your little old well. Thinking, 'Oh, that wall looks very big to me, I have some much room here', and the amazing thing is I think I'm in control. This is my little domain. This is my authoritative situation. I'm the authority around here. So until assistance comes from outside, there's no hope. That is why we go to give out these books! That is why we give *harinama*! That is why we are trying to provide assistance, because it's our obligation. We have had the mercy of the spiritual master.

We are so grateful because our spiritual master has forced open our stupid eyes with the torchlight of knowledge, our darkened eyes. And that knowledge brings responsibility. As soon as you know what truth is you have to become the servant of truth. We are actually a servant of truth. Krishna is truth. Veda means truth and because we have taken from the Vedas we are the servant of the Vedas. It's not a one-sided business that we simply take, take, and take. We have to serve the Vedas because we are taking from them. That is the meaning of affection. If your father is giving you and giving you, then you want to return. Krishna says, 'I am the Vedas, by the Vedas I am to be known, *vedanta krt*. I am the source of the Vedas.'

7: EVERYONE NEEDS THEIR SHELTER

A TALK TO GUESTS AT GLASTONBURY FESTIVAL, UK - JUNE 2000

Once we were on a morning walk with Srila Prabhupada at the beach in Bombay. There were thousands of tiny little crabs and they would run towards the ocean whenever we went near them. Prabhupada stopped with his cane, and explained, 'They feel anxiety and fear and therefore they need shelter, so they take shelter of the big ocean. They are not running towards the bushes. They instinctively know that they will get shelter in the ocean. They know it will give them protection because once they enter the water, they are safe'. I don't know if when you were a child, you used to go on the beach looking for crabs - but as soon as they entered the water, they were gone. They had some mystical way that once they entered the ocean that was it! They almost became one with the huge ocean and went out of sight. You couldn't find them. Prabhupada was saying, 'This is their instinct, they are not running towards the bushes or the land because the Supersoul is guiding them to take shelter in the water'.

Many types of creatures have this amazing type of intuition. There's a rhinoceros that the baby runs away from the mother as soon as it's born. No other child runs away from its mother, but this rhino runs when it is born because otherwise the mother licks the child and kills it. The rhinoceros' tongue is like sandpaper, so the skin of the tiny little creature is taken off. So instinctively, when they are born they disappear for a few days and return when their skin is stronger, in case mummy gives them a lick. That is the Supersoul giving them instruction that, 'You better get some shelter because this mum of yours is going to *whop* off your skin with the nicest of intentions'.

This direction of the Supersoul is called *buddhi or* intelligence. We all have intelligence. Some of us have it more than others, but we all have intelligence. Intelligence is there to guide us. This guidance of the Supersoul is our real shelter. Bhaktisiddhanta said something very nice that, 'By absorbing ourselves in the small, we lose sight of the great'. It is a very profound

56

statement. That is the principle of matter. Matter is a limiting and restricting energy. It restricts us. Everybody thinks that they get freedom by being absorbed in matter. They think that they will become free by taking shelter of the very thing that restricts them. It such a stupid idea!

In other words, I think I will become happy by taking shelter of the very thing that is causing me distress. They don't know what is distressing them. They are not seeing the reality because they are taking shelter of the small. That is called *duratma*. There are two types of people in this world, *duratma* and *mahatma*. *Mahatma* means broad-minded, and *duratma* means small-minded. As the mind becomes more absorbed in the material energy, it becomes pettier and pettier.

We can see this practically. You don't have to be a top scholar in philosophy to know that materialistic people are petty-minded. Like the classical person who is very bodily conscious, always fussing over everything, 'Oh, my hair is not quite right!' Always looking in the mirror, fussing around to get things right. They are absorbed in thinking that the body itself – even if it's the ugliest thing on the planet - can look nice.

So this is called *maya* or illusion. *Maya* takes away our intelligence. This is *maya's* business, to take away our intelligence. Krishna is there to give us intelligence. He says, *ye yatha mam prapadyante*, 'As you approach me, I give you intelligence. As you surrender to me I will give you everything. I have no shortage'. Krishna is not short of anything.

Try to understand that everyone takes shelter of something. Some people take shelter of their family. That is why they rush home at night, thinking, 'When will I get home and see my lovely *coochy woochy* Diana?' She gives me little *cuddly wuddlies* and I will be happy after a stressful day in the office. And then my little *kiddie widdies* will roll all over me and saliva will drip on my head. It's natural. You come home to your family and there's a nice house to go to. You decorate it the way you want. You've got your television in the right place. You've got the games that you play, and your little pipe in the right spot. Everything is just right, and you can put your legs up and relax because you're home. All your anxieties are left at the door... supposedly. We take shelter of our family, friends, our job or our studies. We take shelter of alcohol or raving around and running around having sex.

Prabhupada says, 'Fear arises when a living entity misidentifies himself as the material body because of absorption in the external, illusory energy of the Lord. When the living entity thus turns away from the Supreme Lord, he also forgets his constitutional position as a servant of the Lord'.

By absorbing ourselves in the small, we lose contact with the great. Everyone is absorbed in something petty. We are so embarrassed by our petty world, that we try to look to other worlds or we try to look to others. We broaden our sphere of consciousness by trying to pretend we can move out into the universe and we can expand our field more and more and more.

Prabhupada once gave a very nice example that you may go very high up into the sky but you are always anxious to come back. The astronauts are always thinking, 'When will I go down and see my *cuddly wuddly* Diana, my little baby!' When people go up in an aeroplane, they can't wait to land. As soon as they land, they immediately stand up and pull their bags out. You could say, 'Isn't it such an exciting thing, you are sixty thousand feet up in the air, are you not excited?' Because if you could walk thirty thousand feet up in the sky people would be going, 'Isn't that amazing?', but who wants to stay up there? People want sense gratification. They want to come down and hit the bar and other locations. That's why on the aeroplanes they try to give them all sorts of distractions to absorb them in. They have a television, food all the time and people asking, 'Would you like this? Would you like that?'

People always have to take shelter of something and what are we taking shelter of predominantly? Our mind. We are being conducted through the mind. The mind is the conductor to the material world and the senses are the medium it uses to connect. Electricity is a very powerful energy but you need a conductor and a connector. *Maya* is the energy of the material world and the mind conducts that energy and the senses connect us to the material world.

What are we absorbing ourselves in through the senses? The sense objects. By nature, we have to absorb ourselves in something. The sense objects keep us either happily or miserably absorbed. Sometimes we say, 'Oh I'm happy', and sometimes we say, 'Oh this is a miserable experience'. Krishna says *matra sparsas tu kaunteya sitosna sukha dukha da.* Sometimes we are tasting happiness, sweetness, and when we taste happiness we feel very excited but sometimes within moments, distress comes.

The phenomena of the material world are not substantial to give us proper shelter. You can only have proper shelter when you are happy. That is a fact. The highest principle of happiness is when one is absorbed in love. The principle of love is the highest principle and for the living entity to take shelter, we need to be in love. In the material world, our love is not wholesome. We can love so many things but the very things we are trying to love are not substantial.

If they were substantial, they would give us substantial satisfaction. We can't properly absorb ourselves in something insubstantial. We want to surrender to it and take shelter of it, but the thing we are trying to take shelter of is not substantial because it is the shadow of Krishna. If I want to love you, can I love your shadow? The shadow is the one thing you can't love about someone. You could love almost everything about someone but not their shadow. Let's be honest, you'd have to be really desperately in love with someone to be chasing their shadow.

Maya is the projected energy of Krishna. The shadow proves the substance exists because without substance you can't have a shadow. You can't have an illusion unless there's the reality. You can't have a reflection unless there's an object. The real conclusion has to be, is this reality? *Athato brahma jijnasa.* Now that you are in this human form of life, it is the time to study what reality and illusion are. Krishna says in the *Bhagavad-gita*, 'One who can understand the difference between matter and spirit and the controller of both, is in perfect knowledge'. Matter is prone to change. Everything is changing. Everything is shifting. That very thing which we are trying to absorb ourselves in, is not even substantially there, what to speak of enjoying it. It's not even there. It doesn't even stay.

The first principle of enjoying something or absorbing oneself in something is at least it should stick around. But matter doesn't. It is constantly changing. Your mind in the morning is different from your mind at noontime or in the evening. You can be sitting there thinking, 'Oh! I feel great', and a second later you can be feeling totally miserable. Even though the mind is the conductor of the material world, it is so fickle. That is a fact we cannot argue with. Even psychiatrists will tell you that. We conduct our consciousness through the subtle and then through the gross.

If the subtle itself is constantly changing, that makes life extremely difficult because by this constant change of mind you have a very big problem. This flickering in Sanskrit is called *cancala*. The mind is constantly flickering and changing so that we don't have steady determination in the sense of having faith in something. We have to have faith. That is the first principle of determination, that at least you should have faith in something.

That's why most people one minute they have faith in this and then they have faith in that. They do this and then they do that. They're constantly changing and because of this constant flickering of the mind, there's no peace. How can there be happiness without peace? Internally there is a constant change, and externally the situations are constantly changing. We become subject to the constant changes of matter.

I might be feeling wonderful and then some idiot comes along and punches me in the head or steals my money. You have felt that many times. You're having a great time and then you lose your car keys and then five hours later, you're ready to punch someone. Someone comes up to you and says, 'Are you okay, Prabhu?', and you are totally stressed out because you know everyone is gone but you can't leave. You get this a lot at festivals: we had a great time, wonderful singing, *kirtans*, *prasad* (spiritual food) and then we lost our keys, and we can't go home. There are billions of examples. I'm sure we can all tell a few examples of when we were very happy and then suddenly the circumstances changed. So even though we are happy internally, the externals change and they become our cause of distress.

This is called *klesa* in Sanskrit, meaning these are antagonistic elements. They are inflictions on us. Just like our mind, it's an infliction. We have this thing inside us which is inflicting torment on us. We don't want this but it happens. We don't belong here, we don't belong in this body, we don't belong with this transitory changeable energy. We are suffering on account of the extreme changeability of matter and these outside forces, which are actually hostile to our real happiness. If you study it, you will find that circumstances are the biggest cause of distress. That is why everyone is always trying to find their own little space. Mother Vrinda's got her little van which she hides in, I've got my little van, someone else has their little room, and they practically go in there to hide.

Everyone has to have their shelter and there we can hide away and hopefully not get hit by a tornado or hurricane, and hopefully not going to get bugged by the management or thugs, or whatever comes in. You can hide away there and you can feel protected. Everyone's doing that. Everyone needs their shelter, but we find that even these bigger shelters, like our family, society, home and all the rest of it, also change. They move on with time. Everything is shifting with the forces of time. What is the conclusion? By becoming too absorbed in this transitory material world, we have become very petty. We have become lost to petty activity.

This existence is Krishna's accommodating energy. Although we are Krishna's, and this is Krishna's energy, why are we not seeing Krishna? Because we have separated the energy from the energetic. When you want to enjoy the sunshine you separate it from the sun. Giving a crude example, electricity is present everywhere but you need to get it into the powerhouse and then get your electrical cables, and then bring your light bulbs. Everyone is capturing some situation in this material world. We are capturing our small world within a big world. There's this huge universe but we've captured a little bit of energy. We have a little bit of money in our pocket, our little flat, our little car, our little family, our little unit.

We are trying to separate the energy from the energetic, and this is artificial. The living entity can never actually be separated from Krishna. Krishna manifests Himself through this material energy in order to give us some support. Krishna is the real support. You can see it practically. I need pleasure, so Krishna comes as *anna maya*, which means the pleasure in foodstuffs. Krishna is there in the food. That's why when you bite into a beautiful peach, you feel Krishna. Where is that taste coming from? If it's such a simple thing, how come science hasn't been able to create some new variety? Whatever is here on this planet for our sustenance and our support has been here for millions of years, and it will be here for millions of years in the future. Nothing new has come. Nobody makes anything new. We just come here and manipulate what exists, and we go.

If someone visits your apartment, everything is already there in the apartment. They don't need to bring anything new. If I visit a friend, I don't need to bring my pots and pans, a new cooker, a fridge and a new shower. Everything is already there. I use what's available there and I go. Similarly in this world, we are visitors. We are visiting Krishna's kingdom and Krishna is providing many nice facilities. The sun is there and we take it for granted but the sun is actually wonderfully situated to give us a nice warm back and to give us light. All of this variety is coming from the sun. These arrangements are there. So when we study the arrangement, we see that Krishna is giving us support. And instead of remembering Krishna by His energy, we are forgetting Krishna. That is the problem.

The problem is not the energy, the problem is that due to the contamination of our mind and our false ego we are separating the energy from the energetic. The responsibility of our human form of life, is simply to turn our minds back to Krishna and then everything becomes fully perfect and complete. Krishna is perfect and complete and His energy is perfect and complete. We are also perfect and complete, but our incompleteness is our incomplete understanding, our ignorance of the material world.

Krishna says, 'For those who are constantly devoted to Me and worship Me with all their heart, I give them this extra thing'. We need this extra thing. 'I give them the understanding by which they can come to me'. That is the only missing thing. What is that 'understanding by which they can come to Me?' Krishna says, *patram puspam phalam toyam*, 'Simply you offer to Me with your love and devotion a leaf, a flower, a fruit or water and I will accept it'. Krishna only wants our love. He wants us to turn to Him in love. He doesn't need anything else from us. We have nothing which we can add to Krishna. What are we going to do? Are we going to put more *gopis* in the spiritual world to keep Krishna happy? Or perform some wonderful feat to impress Krishna?

If you try to offer a candle to the sun, it doesn't require your candle. You can't say, 'Hey sun! You look a bit dim today! Do you need a bit of help? Here's a candle!' Similarly with God, we don't need to give anything to God. He's not in need of anything. Rather He's giving everything to everyone. But the only thing He wants is our love because we are linked to Him in our loving relationship and on account of coming into this orbit of the material world, we are becoming more and more entangled. We are constantly chasing after the bubbles in the ocean of the material world. We are constantly chasing after different illusions. But none of them are giving any shelter. We have no shelter in the material world.

As Krishna says, *bahunam janmanam ante*, after many lifetimes of struggling and chasing after this shadow of Krishna, finally we understand, *vasudeva sarvam iti*, He who is behind the shadow. The real substance is beyond that shadow. The real substance is Krishna. We need to connect up to the reality. When the clouds are covering the sun, you can't get a complete experience, something is missing. When you wake up in the morning and it's all cloudy and miserable, there's something missing in your life. You feel a bit dismal. But when the sun comes out then you feel very invigorated. The natural condition of the daytime is sunshine. If you go up in an aeroplane you will see the sun is always there. It didn't go anywhere. It's always there. We are in the cloudy material world and therefore we are feeling very dismal. This is natural because we are not in our real position. When we come to this plane of Krishna consciousness - we are back home, back to Godhead. Then we think, 'Now I am home, I can take real shelter'.

Krishna is substantial because He is unlimited. What is His unlimited potency? *Ananda mayo bhyasat*. He has unlimited pleasure. Krishna's entire creation is full of pleasure. You can't understand that materially, because there is no pleasure here. The shadow does not have grapes. If you go to a grapevine and there's a shadow, you can't enjoy grapes from the shadow. You'd look pretty stupid trying to pick some grapes from the shadow. Or you'd look stupid if there's a reflection of a mango tree in the river and you dive into the river looking for mangos. But that doesn't mean there aren't any mangos or there are no grapes. It's just that you've found the shadow. Everything that is here, is there, but in the complete form of *sat cit ananda*.

In the material world, there are two things: matter and spirit. But they don't mix properly with each other. Just like your body and you are not mixing. You're trying to mix up with your body but in actuality, you can't because it is made up of matter. It is just some dead earth and water. There's no essential relationship between you and your body. If you pull out your intestines, do you have a relationship with them? It's a machine. The body is a machine. It's like trying to have a relationship with a car. The relationship we want is when it functions for your benefit. When the body functions for your benefit, then you have a relationship with it. When it stops functioning for your benefit, you try to get rid of it. Like suicide, people cut their necks because the body is no longer doing what they want it to. That's the material world, the shadow.

When it's giving you some pleasure you think it's a great place, but when it's not cooperating with you (as non-cooperation is its real quality), 'Oh, suicide! Let me get out of here!' We want *moksha,* liberation. When you've got an extreme stomach ache or cancer, or when your ears are falling off or when your teeth are falling into your food, then you're embarrassed. You bite an apple and there are four teeth left in it, you think, 'What's going on here? This is getting serious!'

Matter is only good when it cooperates with you. You are not the lord of matter. Do you understand? You cannot force it to cooperate. It may or may not cooperate. Whether it cooperates or not, that's your good luck or bad luck. If you put a hundred pounds on a horse to come in first - if it wins you feel great but if it comes in last because it fell over at the last fence, you're crying.

Just like here at Glastonbury Festival some cooperation is there, but then people overdo it. They take so much alcohol that they're drunk, falling over and banging their head. Cooperation is the real thing. We've come here to try and make matter cooperate with us and to subject it to our will. But that's not the reality. If matter was conscious, it would take the initiative. But because matter is dead, it doesn't take the initiative. Therefore, it's a struggle. When you want to enjoy it, you've got to do all the work. You don't want your body to get old because you want to have a good time, but it gets old. It doesn't cooperate with you because it doesn't have initiative. It doesn't see that you want it to stay young. Why? Because it's made up of dead elements. Even though you want to be young, the body doesn't have any initiative. It just works according to outside forces.

Sometimes with a little hard work, you get matter to cooperate with you and you feel proud. 'Oh, I've got something here'. You feel as proud as a peacock. But when it isn't cooperating with us, what are we trying to do? We are trying to subject matter to our desires. But it will never be subjected to us because it controls us. Matter is the energy of Krishna. The only way that you can get matter to function properly is to use it in Krishna's service. Then it becomes glorious, as glorious as it can. Matter is always a bad bargain. As Prabhupada said, 'Make the best use of a bad bargain'. Get this bag of skin and bone and stool and everything else, and use it to serve Krishna.

8: WHY WE'RE RESTRICTED IN THE MATERIAL WORLD

A SUNDAY FESTIVAL CLASS AT ISKCON BIRMINGHAM, UK

Bhagavad-gita 3.27

The spirit soul bewildered by the influence of false ego thinks himself the doer of activities that are in actuality carried out by the three modes of material nature.

Purport

Two persons, one in Krishna consciousness and the other in material consciousness, working on the same level, may appear to be working on the same platform, but there is a wide gulf of difference in their respective positions. The person in material consciousness is convinced by false ego that he is the doer of everything. He does not know that the mechanism of the body is produced by material nature, which works under the supervision of the Supreme Lord. The materialistic person has no knowledge that ultimately he is under the control of Krishna. The person in false ego takes all credit for doing everything independently, and that is the symptom of his nescience. He does not know that this gross and subtle body is the creation of material nature, under the order of the Supreme Personality of Godhead, and as such his bodily and mental activities should be engaged in the service of Krishna, in Krishna consciousness. The ignorant man forgets that the Supreme Personality of Godhead is known as Hrisikesa, or the master of the senses of the material body, for due to his long misuse of the senses in sense gratification, he is factually bewildered by the false ego, which makes him forget his eternal relationship with Krishna.

Along with intelligence comes the power of discrimination. Although our bodies are animal-like, we no longer have an animal life because we have responsibility. What is the meaning of responsibility? Think about it - the ability to respond. If you can't respond then you're not responsible are you? If a man commits a crime whilst being intoxicated, he may go to court and say, 'Your honour I was drunk! I didn't know I hit that fellow with the bottle! I thought it was a newspaper in my hand'. He may try to get out of the responsibility by saying, 'I was intoxicated'. Someone may say, 'I murdered my wife's lover because I couldn't control it, out of anger'. There's a term for that - a crime of passion. In some countries, you can be freed on the grounds of a crime of passion. One may be too angry because of passion. You can say, 'I was not responsible'. In law, it's called diminished responsibility. A child cannot be put in the same category because their responsibility is diminished, the child doesn't yet have an adequate development of intelligence to distinguish between right and wrong.

What is the basis of responsibility? It's based on knowledge. That's why we need knowledge and education. In some cultures, they cook and eat their grandfathers. It's a culturally accepted activity. In those cultures, there's nothing wrong with it at all. The reason it happens is that they don't have adequate knowledge. Some people eat animals and say, 'Oh, I don't know. I just eat them. It's not my fault, I buy them at the supermarket, at ASDA. So blame them, not me! I'm just eating it!'

So this science of *Bhagavad-Gita* is very important because as Krishna says, 'This knowledge is the king of all education because it gives direct perception to the self through realization'. There are different types of knowledge, and *vijnana* or realized knowledge, is that knowledge which is not relative to the body. In the material world, all knowledge is relative. Relative means dependent. You have your relatives. They're your dependents or you're their dependents. The child is relative to the father and mother and the child is also dependent upon the father and mother. The child is not independent. Later on at a certain stage, the child can become independent.

In reality, we are all dependent. I'm dependent on water, air and food. I'm dependent upon my health and so many things. If you study your body, it has many dependencies. You're dependent on money. As Chanakya Pandit says, 'If a man doesn't have money in this world, everything is vacant'. Nowadays nobody wants someone with no money because money is the honey. If we have honey you can have you some sweetness. So we are also dependent on money. We're dependent on the government. If the government is corrupt, we become disturbed: 'They're taking too much tax!' They're squeezing the people with taxes and people are crying. Every year, more and more tax but nothing changes. They are taking tax, squeezing our blood, but nothing has changed. If you go to a hospital and they keep taking pints of blood out of you, but you keep getting sicker and sicker, what is the point? So we are also forcibly dependent on the government.

Krishna is pointing out that we are dependent on nature. Nature provides us different types of bodies and they function according to the laws of nature. The laws of nature say that everyone dies by a hundred years old. The odd person lives over a hundred, but otherwise, 'Everyone out! Your time's up! Get out!' You can construct a big skyscraper and live in it, but within a few years, you have to get out of your body. Why? Because the next lot has to come in. The old crow has to make way for the new crow. The old crow is there eating everything and the new crow can't get anything, so the new crow pushes the old crow out of the way.

In life we are running after many things, but then all of a sudden you find that you have to get out. We have a particular body according to *guna* (nature) and *karma (activities)*. We have been doing activities since time immemorial and we have a particular type of result. Some of us have a nice body due to good *karma*. Some have a mediocre body due to mediocre *karma*. And some have a not so nice body due to bad *karma*. Otherwise, how do you explain the varieties of manifestations? You can't explain that everything is accidental. Nature is dependent, not independent. In the Sanskrit language, one of the words for nature is *prakrti* and it means that which is dependent. Nature is dependent on laws. That's why we say the 'laws' of nature. Anything which works under laws means it is dependent on the laws.

Prakrti is the energy, but what is the energetic? *Prakrti* is not independent. Your body is not independent, it is dependent upon consciousness. It is useless with the absence of consciousness. Even a big president like Kennedy, he was sitting in a car one minute and the next minute he was gone. His body became useless because death had come. Nature has a support like my body has a support. The thing which supports nature is called *purusa*, the energetic. Prabhupada gives a very simple example, if someone is hitting you with a stick, who is to blame, the person or the stick? Do you tell the police, 'I want that stick arrested because it hit me!' No. Maybe that's a fair argument that the stick hurt me, therefore the stick should be arrested. If we look a little bit deeper we see that yes, the stick is beating me but who is holding the stick? That's more important. When you plead - you're pleading to the person holding the stick. It's no good talking to a stick. People would think you're mad.

So, therefore, energy and the energetic are simultaneously one and yet different. There are two aspects of reality, the energetic and the energy. And energy has two aspects, the superior energy (*para*) and inferior energy (*apara*). Your body is a mixture of the superior and inferior energies. For example, your hair is inferior, if you chop your hair off, you don't want to keep it and put it in a bag. Most people don't hang on to their loose hair as it is useless. So hair is only good when it's connected with the body. If you have a very beautiful girlfriend but every time you have soup you find her hair in it, you wouldn't like it. She may have beautiful hair but you don't want it in your soup. So when the hair is connected with the body it has a superior arrangement and when it's disconnected it is inferior. Similarly, when our body is connected with the soul it has a superior arrangement, but when it is separated from the soul it becomes an inferior arrangement.

Krishna is *govindam adi purusam*, the supreme controller and the supreme creator, maintainer and destroyer. He is governing everything and we can only experience a little bit of His energy. One manifestation of God's energy is in the form of food. So you may say, 'I like God in the form of food, so I'm going to eat a mountain of food', but you can only eat a small amount of food. Even if you're rich, you can only eat a few pieces of bread. Although it is the energy of God, you are very tiny, so you can only know and experience a small part of God's energy.

The energy is regulated by the control of the energetic. This can be understood in a higher sense that God is the energetic and He regulates all the energy. All of us are regulated by that energy. Life means regulations - birth, old age, disease and death. You may say, 'I don't want those regulations! For me, there's no old age!' People will say you're crazy because you are regulated by time. Time is regulating how much you can enjoy. You may be a billionaire like Bill Gates. Billy has a lot of money but will he live to enjoy it all? That's the problem. He may want to enjoy it but he's regulated by time. Even if he is willing to spend twenty billion dollars to buy another minute of life, he won't get it. You can't buy time. You can't buy many things because they're not within our spending power. They are controlled by a higher authority - nature.

Like if a child is naughty, they show them the stick. Why? To regulate the child. 'Behave, otherwise the stick is there!' You must never hit children but you can show them it's there. So when they see the stick they say, 'Oh I don't want to argue with that'. Nature is like that. Nature is like a stick. It is regulating you, 'Behave yourself! Don't be a nonsense! Don't drink too much! Otherwise you will end up in the gutter'. Many people like to drink a lot, but end up in the gutter because they misbehave. Or you may say, 'I like to eat a lot!' But then you become fat or you get heart problems. So even though people love eating, they have to regulate it. Similarly, people love smoking and they like sex, but there are so many things saying, 'Okay, you want to do this too much? Then I'll punish you!' So you can have a little bit. Prabhupada used to say, salt is very nice, but if you put too much it's suffering. If you put a whole kilo of salt in your food then what is the use?

Krishna is not saying 'don't enjoy' but He is saying - you must regulate your enjoyment. But why should it be regulated? Nobody likes regulations. It's like one person said, 'Everything I like is either prohibited, bad for you or criminal'. Many things we like are not allowed by the government or by social and moral restrictions. Why are all these restrictions there? We are restricted because we don't belong here. Krishna is restricting us to let us know we don't belong here. When someone goes to prison, he's put under certain restrictions. But they lift them as soon as he walks out of the door and is released. Why are there restrictions in prison? Is it to be vindictive or to cause anxiety? Is it to be torturous? No, the idea of restriction is to let that person know that you don't belong here and don't come back. That's the idea.

Similarly, you should understand that the material energy is a restricting energy. That is why it's called the limiting energy of God. It's to restrict the living entities that are rebellious of God. 'Do you want to carry on independently without Me? At least I will show you that you cannot exist happily like that.' Sometimes a son wants to be independent or wants his due money from the father. But the father thinks, 'No, if I give him all the money now, he will surely do some nonsense with it', so the father restricts it and puts it in a trust. 'Every year you will get a small quantity of the money'. You love your child but you know that this child will misuse the money. The idea of a trust is to regulate the flow of money. Otherwise the child may waste time getting intoxicated. Similarly, in spiritual life there are regulations but they are not there simply for the sake of it, but they are there so that one can practice spiritual life properly.

The body functions according to material laws but the soul functions according to spiritual freedom. That's why there are two words in Sanskrit, *mahatma* and *duratma*. *Mahatma* means one who is broad-minded and *duratma* means one who is narrow-minded. When you take shelter of the material energy it makes you narrower. It restricts you more and more. That's why animal life means more restrictions. What's the difference between human and animal? More restrictions. We are living in comfort. We're not living in the field like the animals. If we sit in a field every night in the freezing cold we'll be crying, but an animal can sit there because he is more restricted. He doesn't think of going to Hawaii or Disneyland or going out to the pub. If he did he'd go mad. Suppose all of his life he was standing there thinking, 'I could have caught an aeroplane and gone to the Taj Mahal, but instead I'm here eating grass and getting cold'. He doesn't think like that.

The body is manifested from consciousness. So the more you become implicated in material energy the more your consciousness becomes degraded. You get different types of body according to your degradation or elevation. If you always want to sleep then you get a body which is good for sleeping. A bear can hibernate for six months a year. If you like a lot of sex, you can have a body where sex is had every five minutes. Or if you like to swim in the water, you can get a fish body.

There are many millions of different permutations of matter and these are all different forms of restriction. Material happiness is not a liberated thing, it's a restricted thing. Many people think that material happiness means freedom, but it doesn't - it means more restriction. The more you try to exploit material energy, the more you become implicated in reactions. That is called *karma*.

The sages of yore are teaching us that instead of becoming a servant of the senses, one must become a master of the senses. One must become a master within the body. The body is like a city with different gates. The gates are the eyes, ears, nostrils, mouth, anus and the genitals. And what comes in the gates? Sense gratification. So you have to be the master and control what is coming in, making sure that you don't become overly bewildered by sense objects.

Now, why would you want to control it? Because one has to understand, *athato brahma jijnasa* - I am not material, I am spiritual. Without that principle the whole society is useless. Spirituality is like having a one before all the zeros. Unless you have a one before all of the zeros it's useless. You may say I'm a very rich man, I have fifty million zeros in my bank account, but if there's not a *one* before them, it's useless.

Similarly, unless you put the energetic principle first, the energy itself becomes inferior. Noughts are inferior and superior means one. *Eka bahunam* means the one among many, the original Supreme Personality of Godhead, Krishna. When you put Krishna there everything becomes unlimitedly meaningful. The energy is to be enjoyed by the energetic. Energy means that which is created by the energetic. Why do parents have a child? Because there's pleasure in bringing up a child and seeing the child grow. That child is a source of happiness for the family. Sex life gives pleasure and from that pleasure comes another pleasure, children. It can be misery sometimes but it is also pleasure. In the same way, we are created by God for pleasure.

In a relationship with a child, at some point, you give the child independence. The child can decide, 'I no longer want to please my family by serving them, I want to be the enjoyer'. When a child becomes an enjoyer in a family then the problem starts. Because the father's car goes missing, his money goes missing and everything goes missing. The father says, 'Hey son! What's going on here?' And the son says, 'Hey dad, it's my turn to enjoy now! You can go to the old people's home'.

We are to be enjoyed by Krishna, but enjoyed doesn't mean it's one way. It means reciprocation. But if we want to be independent, Krishna says, 'Here's your independence, take it'. But because we're minute, we can only take a minute part. The son can't take everything, he can take whatever is the allocated amount from his father. The son may say to the father, 'Dad I want everything and you get lost', but that's not possible. 'Son, it's not your property, it's my property! You take this amount and go'. You come to an arrangement.

When the living entity wants to be independent of Krishna, Krishna says, 'Okay, here is your arrangement', the material arrangement. An intelligent person can understand that this inferior arrangement is inadequate. Everything about this world is inadequate. This is Krishna's mercy. It's designed like that so the living entity will understand without God everything is inadequate. When the sun is not there, you may have so many candles but it's inadequate. Suppose you decide that your candle is very powerful and you stand above the ocean and light up the ocean. Your candle is very tiny, so it's natural for the small to identify with the great. But the small can never become the great. Everybody wants to be great. But to be great and want to be great there's a vast difference. The candle cannot light up the world. But when the sun comes immediately everything is lit without any effort and your candle becomes useless.

Similarly, our independence is very tiny, but we think it's very important. 'I'm such a big man, I'm so important, I have so much money and followers.' But in comparison to God, it is nothing. We are sitting on one planet amongst billions of planets. And within this universe, our planet is only a piece of dust. And within this one planet, there are so many countries. And we are sitting in one little country England, it is only a small island. And on that island, there are so many cities, towns and villages. And of those, there's one place called Birmingham. Within that, there are so many districts in Birmingham. And within those districts, there are so many houses. And within those houses, there are so many rooms. And in one room we are sitting there, thinking that everything is happening by our arrangement.

This is the nature of the ego. We think that everything exists in relation to our existence. But in actuality, everything exists on our head. We are a servant of everything. Nobody wants to be a servant of God, because they think that that's a weakness. We prefer to serve our body. But what's the last thing the body does? It lets you down. There's a joke about the undertaker: he's the last guy to finally let you down and put you in the grave. You serve your body, day and night looking after it, making sure it gets nice things. But then, what does it do? It gradually becomes more and more invalidated by time. And it becomes more and more useless. Krishna says, 'Don't simply serve the body'. Serve Krishna. Then everything will be perfect.

There are two things. Either you're dominated or you're a dominator. Nature is dominating your body. You can say, 'I am the dominator of my body'. So then think of all of the functions going on in the body. Which ones are the ones that you chose to do? They go on whether you want them or not. That means you're not the dominator. To be the dominator means to be the controller and the creator. People think that dominating means when I'm enjoying myself. But if you study the so-called enjoyment of the body, they are all dependencies, not enjoyments. Real enjoyment can't be a dependency. Do you understand that point? So as soon as you're dominated by something, that is your dominator. So in order to be a dominator or to be a controller or to be God, you need to be independent.

Krishna is described as *janmady asya yatah*, that from which everything emanates, and *cartesu abhijna svarat*, absolutely independent and cognizant. We are not fully conscious. If we were then we would have some quality of domination. If we were the dominator of the body, we would know how many hairs we have on our head. But only God knows that. You can say this is my body, but which thing inside the body do you like to keep the most? What is it that's so great about the body? You cannot keep any of it.

The body is a machine made up of different functions. It's created by someone else to function in a certain way. You didn't create the body. You don't function on your own independence. Nobody can say, 'I have to spend a lot of money on food, so I'll stop eating'. We can't do that. We can't stop sleeping. We can't stop fearing. We can't stop the sufferings of the mind, body and other living entities. Everything about us is totally dependent.

We have to search out that person who is independent. That is the search for God. When you study God in any religion, He should be independent. He can't also be dependent. If God is dependent on government hand-outs or social security, or if God is dependent upon something within His creation, then that is not independent. That would mean whatever He's dependent upon is God.

There is no greater controller than the *isvara parama*. *Parama* means supreme and *isvara* means controller. Krishna means that Personality who is the Supreme Controller. Even though God is unlimited He has the unlimited power to be a person. That is a great thing to understand. How can the unlimited become a person? We are limited, so we cannot understand how there could be an unlimited person. When we talk about *purusa*, we mean the cause of all causes. Just like, a man who creates a company is the enjoyer of the company because he created it and controls it. If you get a job in a company and say, 'Hey you, managing director! Get out of here! I'm taking over today', you'd probably last five minutes. Because he is the owner of the company. It doesn't matter who you think you are.

One might argue that man is very intelligent because he also creates things. But what is he creating? A mess. Nature has already done everything. But they're thinking, 'Oh we're so intelligent! We will create something!' But they just create a mess. The rivers are pure, so they pollute them. The air is pure, they pollute it. Their bodies are pure, they pollute them. Their society structure, they pollute it. They pollute everything. And then when it's all a big mess, what do they do? They kill each other.

They are not even to be called enjoyers in the simplest sense. An enjoyer is someone who can actually enjoy. It seems like we're enjoying, but we're not. What we're doing is giving pleasure to the senses through material objects. Both the senses and the objects are totally out of our control. That's why we try to control the air, the land, music, buildings, aesthetics - we try to control all of these things to bring them into our service in a measurable amount that we can enjoy. Like water is very enjoyable, but not if you have a hundred million gallons in your room you cannot enjoy it. But God can. That's the difference. Because He's God. If you want to measure God, then you have to study *Srimad Bhagavatam*. Because everything Krishna does is immeasurable.

Actually, suffering is His kindness, His mercy. Therefore *maya* is called the affection of God. The only reason people turn to God is because of suffering. Practically speaking ninety-nine per cent of all people turn to God because of suffering. There are very few cases in the history of mankind of people turning to God because they became a Mr Rockefeller or a big businessman. All the great Saints were poor. What were the Six Goswamis wearing? Simple pieces of cloth. Look on the altar, how many people are wearing little bits of cloth? Most of them. But how many rich people are coming? How many politicians are coming? Therefore Krishna gives us suffering to make us wake up and realise.

The material world is like fire. The mother is saying, 'Child, don't touch the fire!' But the child is saying, 'No! I'll touch it! I want to touch it. It looks nice. It glitters'. But when he touches the fire, he won't touch it again. So material nature is there to awaken you. You may think, 'This is a very harsh awakening! It is the mercy of God'. What has happened in this life is preparing you for the next. It's not a one life show. You may go through millions of lives. But the ultimate goal of nature is to take you back to Godhead. Nature is created to take you back to home back to Godhead.

Nature is testing you, to see how determined you are to leave this place. When people say, 'I am very happy in this place', then that's a curse. If someone says, 'I hope you become happy and wealthy and have a big house in Hawaii', it's a curse. You should reply, 'Why are you cursing me?' But if someone says, 'I hope you lose everything and only get God,' that's a blessing. People used to come to Prabhupada and say, 'Swamiji, please give me your blessings', and he'd say, 'If I gave you my blessings, you'd become annoyed'. They'd say, 'No, no, Swamiji, you give me!'
'Okay, lose everything and become a devotee of Krishna.'
'Oh no, Swamiji! Don't give me that one! Give me the other one that says that I'll be rich.'

Everybody wants something big in this world, something substantial. But they don't know the only substantial thing is God. This world is not substantial. If I give you a room full of money, it's only paper. It's not substantial. Your mind is pacified, 'I have a whole room full of ten million pounds, something substantial has happened to me'. But nothing substantial has happened. Because if you're hungry, you can't eat one piece of paper! So what is substantial? Food? But food comes from God. Is your family substantial? Your family comes from God. There's no chemical company that produces food.

There's no chemical company that produces children or anything. Everything in nature comes from God. So why not search out God? Why search for these other things? Don't settle for little drops of rain in a desert if you want to quench your thirst - go to the rain cloud. We are coming into this world to enjoy, but we don't know where the enjoyment comes from. Prabhupada gave the example of the scorpion and the rice. The scorpion lays its eggs deep inside the bag of rice and when the baby scorpion comes out of the rice people think it was born from the rice. Similarly, because we are living in this world, we're thinking that happiness is born out of worldly things. But nothing comes out of the world except by the arrangement of Krishna. So it's better to inquire about Krishna.

Audience member: So does that mean we are all just *trying* to be happy? People think, 'I'll be happy in Hawaii with that house', or whatever. But you're saying that the enjoyment with Krishna is higher or better?

Tribhuvanatha: There's no enjoyment in the material world. The temporary so-called enjoyment of the material world is very inferior. It's not real enjoyment. For instance, have you ever had eczema? If you are very itchy, when you scratch yourself, you think, 'Oh, this is lovely! I'm having a nice scratch', but you can't say that is a superior enjoyment. If someone says to you, 'How did you enjoy your day yesterday?', and you said, 'I had a great scratch' they would say, 'What sort of enjoyment is that?'

In the material world, we're suffering and when we get relief we say, 'Oh, enjoyment has come!' A person is suffering all day, and then he goes to the pub and has another suffering, a drink, and he thinks, 'Oh I'm really enjoying myself'. He gets carried home in an ambulance. 'I had such a great night, last night. I don't remember what happened'. They are simply replacing one type of suffering with another suffering. When you get relief from that suffering, you think 'I'm enjoying'. So the next day he says, 'I enjoyed myself because I didn't go to the pub! Last night I ended up in the hospital! It's all craziness. This is not enjoyment.

Someone thinks, 'I'll enjoy myself and find a nice girl and marry her'.
If you ask him, 'Why are you in the pub?'
He'll say, 'To get away from my wife'.
'But you married her to enjoy yourself'.
'Yes, but now I'm enjoying getting away from her nagging'.
This is not enjoyment but escape. It's a form of relief. If you're hungry you
say, 'I ate a big meal, I enjoyed myself'. No, your body is hungry, that's why
you're eating. It's not enjoyment, its relief. It is not enjoyment in the real
sense. It's trickery. *Ma-ya* means not-this. It only appears to be real. You may
say you obtain your pleasure from the body. But if you dissect the body and
hang it up, which part is giving you the most pleasure? It is all just tubes and
pipes and other body parts. You can't say, 'This kidney gave me so much
pleasure last year. So I wish I had eight kidneys'. Because it's simply a
machine made up of matter. You're sitting in a machine. Just like you're going
along the motorway in a car you're feeling very happy. As soon as the
steering wheel goes, you're feeling fear and pain but just before you hit the
wall, you escape and think, 'Oh, I'm happy now! Because I would have been
dead! Now I feel happy!' That is not happiness. You're simply being thrown
around by the laws of nature.

One man's food is another man's poison. The cockroach is happy to eat a little
food off of the floor. But what sort of happiness is that? Do you want to do
that? He's happy - his belly is full and he goes home and sleeps with his wife.
The same thing is going on in every body. But you are thinking, 'I'm enjoying
better than the cockroach. I'm eating at a nice table in my room, watching Sky
TV. He hasn't got Sky TV'. But even if you give him Sky TV, what will he do
with it? A cockroach doesn't watch Sky TV. Your enjoyment is different to his
because he has a different body. But it doesn't mean you have superior
enjoyment. You're happy with a big plate of food and he's happy with a few
grains, but that doesn't mean your enjoyment is superior. His belly also
becomes full. He also sleeps. He also has a wife and grandmothers and a
family. He has all of the things you have. He has a little hut inside the wall,

living by the radiator. He lives rent-free. He has no credit cards, he hasn't borrowed money from the bank. When he goes out, he's just looking around and food comes. He feels happy.

So you may say, 'I'm so superior to him', but in actuality, all bodies that exist in this world are dependent on something. And if they're getting that something they think they're happy. But that's not happiness. That is called 'conditional' life. That's all. And you exist within those conditions. All you're doing is moving with that force of energy and you come and you disappear like on a stage. So many insects come out at night and they are flying around, *buzzing,* and in the morning they're dead. Who cares? It was a big fuss at night. 'Wow! Millions of insects are flying around.' But by the morning it's all quiet again. Like a stage show. Neither was it important what they were doing nor is it important that they stopped. It's just part of nature's arrangement. So you come into this world, make a big fuss and go out. Nobody cares that you came, and nobody cares that you went. When you are gone, who cares? Your mum may cry, maybe she's not there. Your father may cry, maybe he'll not be there. Who's there? How many people have gone from this world? Who really knows where they came from, why they came, what they did and where they went to?

9: THE FORMULA FOR PEACE

A LECTURE GIVEN AT A SUNDAY FESTIVAL AT
ISKCON BIRMINGHAM - SUMMER OF 2000

Bhagavad-gita 5.29

Krishna says: A person in full consciousness of Me, knowing Me to be the ultimate beneficiary of all sacrifices and austerities, the Supreme Lord of all planets and demigods, and the benefactor and well-wisher of all living entities, attains peace from the pangs of material miseries.

Purport

The conditioned souls within the clutches of the illusory energy are all anxious to attain peace in the material world. But they do not know the formula for peace, which is explained in this part of the Bhagavad-gita.

Everyone in the material world wants peace. In India, they say, *'shanti, om shanti'*. So *shanti*, peacefulness is sought after by everyone. Even here in the city of Birmingham people have their little house with a little garden. They want to have some seclusion in their small area. In each and every room of their flat or house, they are surrounded by things which are conducive to their peace and happiness. Everybody wants to be peaceful and happy. The reason that we emphasize peace is because everyone in the material world is disturbed and when there is disturbance then it is not possible to be peaceful.

If there's too much noise, our mind becomes agitated. When we're too hungry, we become agitated. When we're too poor, we become agitated. If there is too much or too little of something, we become agitated. If there's too much heat or too little heat, we become disturbed. Therefore we can understand that we exist under certain conditions. These are called material conditions. Prabhupada says the 'conditioned' souls. What is the meaning of 'conditioned' souls? Souls that exist under certain conditions.

Sometimes when the conditions are favourable, we feel very happy and enlivened. If we are experiencing pleasure, the mind becomes very satisfied.

82

Many people take shelter of different types of pleasures. Some people take pleasure in intoxication. They drink good rum and people call each other a 'jolly sailor'. They talk a lot and they sometimes want to dance or they want to tell their life story. They become very relaxed. Even if they go into the bar in a miserable condition, as soon as they've had a few good shots of rum then everyone becomes their friend. Sometimes when people get intoxicated they want to buy everyone a drink, 'Hey you! Have a drink on me! I'm happy now. Before I wasn't happy. Now I have become happy because I have some good liquor in my blood'.

Despite all of the material pleasures, the reality is that the body is always giving us suffering. Krishna says that the experiences of the body are both pleasure and pain, but they are mostly pain as pleasure doesn't come very often. By studying this world, an intelligent person can see that the material world is a hostile environment. This hostility is opposed to our happiness. If someone is hostile to you, their hostility may come in many forms. Sometimes you don't get on with your neighbour. Sometimes there's hostility in the family. There's even hostility amongst countries.

What is the meaning of hostility? It is something inimical to you. When you have an enemy they're hostile to you. The material energy is the enemy of the soul. But we are not thinking of it as such. This is called *maya*. *Maya* means illusion, or literally 'not this'. We think that somehow or other the material energy will bring about a state of happiness and peacefulness. All of us want to make a permanent settlement here. We want to sustain our existence. We don't want to be temporary. If you ask anyone about their idea of happiness, they would say gladly that they want it to be permanent. They do not simply want happiness to come between ten and eleven o'clock. Happiness is not something that we want in short measures. We want it unlimitedly. If there was an idea of unlimited happiness we would certainly be interested in such a proposal.

So, therefore, you find that in every level of human existence, in every philosophy, in every religion, in every actual intelligent proposition, there is some idea of gaining something. We're always in need of gain. We are always in need of help from outside. That is the meaning of conditioned life.

Krishna says *mamaivamso jiva loke jiva bhutah sanatanah manah sasthani indriyani prakrti sthani karsati,* 'The living entities are My part and parcels. They are in Me and they are Mine but due to conditional life they are struggling very hard with the six senses which include the mind'.
The struggle is the interaction between the senses and the sense objects. This is the great struggle of existence. We want to capture these objects of material life and bring them under our jurisdiction to get an experience. If you study it, material life is a life of inexperience. Children have very little experience and knowledge of life, so they listen. They don't have adequate knowledge. They don't have an adequate situation. Children can accept their inadequacy because they know it's foolish to think that they can sustain themselves alone, in terms of food, clothing, accommodation or knowledge. So we are born inadequate and born with inexperience. When we grow up, we are always trying to expand our experience. As Prabhupada quoted very nicely in the beginning of the *Happening* album, he said, 'The materialistic demeanour cannot possibly stretch to the transcendental autocrat, who is ever inviting the fallen conditioned souls to associate with Him through devotion, or eternal serving mood. The phenomenal attractions are often found to tempt sentient beings to enjoy the variegated position'.

Temptation comes through the mind and the senses. We always want to have higher experiences of the mind and the senses. We are experiencing some taste but we always want to have better food. Therefore, there are so many restaurants. If you go to any city there are so many restaurants. There are so many due to different experiences, tastes and smells. There are huge megastores where they sell all varieties of products. What is the meaning of the word mega? Mega means huge. Everything should be mega, very big because we want to always have more and more experience.

The material phenomenon is often found to tempt sentient beings. We want to have more and more of a sentient experience. We want to have more and more of a conscious experience. The problem is we are trying to have a conscious experience of an unconscious world. Matter is dead, it is unconscious. The struggle is that the material energy is the inferior energy but we are from a superior energy. Our existence is superior. So we always want something superior. This struggle of life is to reach the superior experience. We are undergoing this inferior experience. Just like they have the term 'inferiority complex'. We have had so many inferior experiences that we become full of it in our heart. Some people have an inferiority complex and others have a superiority complex. So these two things, superiority and inferiority have to be studied. Because as Krishna says, 'I have two natures, the superior and inferior'.

Unfortunately in the material world, people are identifying with one energy - the inferior energy. They are very much engrossed in the inferior energy. We are also inferior. I can understand that I'm inferior. My body is inferior. My mind is inferior. My senses are inferior. Therefore I have four defects - the tendency to make mistakes, to cheat, being defective in knowledge and being subjected to illusion. These four defects are there in every living creature in this world.

You'll find that those who have a superior condition are lording it over and exploiting those with an inferior condition. This is described in the Srimad Bhagavatam: *jivo jivasya jivanam*. There are 8,400,000 types of living entities and the law of material nature is that one life subsists on another. Those who have legs eat those who don't have legs. Grass has no legs to run away, so the cow eats it. Plants are living, they have a very small amount of consciousness. Subhash Candra Bose found in his scientific tests that plants also have consciousness. But that consciousness is very limited and therefore it is exploited by things which have more consciousness. We can see that because the human being has the greatest level of consciousness, humans are engaged in the greatest amount of exploitation - exploiting the rivers, the land and the sky. A superior country is exploiting an inferior country. One superior individual is exploiting a group of inferior individuals. This is the law of material nature. Wherever you go in the material world you will find that people with superior intelligence always exploit those with inferior intelligence.

This microphone is inferior because I can use it for my use. The microphone is not using me - I am using it. If the microphone was dictating to me what to speak, you'd be surprised. The microphone is inferior therefore it is utilized in my service. Of course, we are utilizing it in Krishna's service. We are utilizing it because it is inferior. Similarly, there is so much wood in this room, why is wood being utilized for our purpose? Because it couldn't run away. If trees could run, they'd run away from all of these people trying to cut them down. They would be running in the forest hiding behind rocks. Cutting trees would be a very difficult thing. Dull matter is always exploited by superior matter.

Therefore, Krishna says, 'Earth, water, fire, air, ether, mind, intelligence and ego - they constitute My inferior energy. But above this, there is My superior energy'. Those who have good intelligence are utilizing the water. This building is made up of brick and water, mixed with fire. Earth is inanimate, so we can mould it into certain forms and shapes that we desire. We can make big skyscrapers and beautiful houses. We can bring in so many different things, plaster, glass and we can have nice curtains on the wall. None of these things could run away as they don't have the sentient ability to protect themselves.

On a further level, in all of these houses the people are bringing in dead goats, cows and sheep to put in their belly. They go to big supermarkets with rows and rows of chopped up bodies. They exploit the animals. But you don't find human bodies in the supermarket because a human will fight back. He can fight back, he's too intelligent for them. If I want to eat human beings, it will be a very difficult task. But to eat a cow, sheep or a goat, it is not so difficult. In the slaughterhouse, the animals queue up. The sheep are waiting to be slaughtered. 'Next one! Next one! Next one!' Then while they're waiting to be slaughtered, they are munching on a little grass. They're taking their last little nibble before they go to their death. They don't have a superior development of intelligence to protect themselves. So the more the development of consciousness, the more there is a tendency towards exploitation.

So this verse of the *Bhagavad-gita* is very important, *bhokataram yajna tapasam,* the Supreme Personality of Godhead is describing a person in full consciousness. There are different levels of consciousness. Nobody has full consciousness. The mind cannot ascertain fullness. If you try to enter into your mind's fullness you cannot. Your mind does not have full knowledge. It's not conceivable to have full knowledge. You can't even entertain the idea of full knowledge. You don't have anything in full, everything is partial. You have some partial knowledge and you have some partial happiness. You might have a little bit of everything. You may say, 'I have money'. But you don't have all the money. You may say, 'I have knowledge', but you don't have all the knowledge. You may say, 'I have a life of experience', but you don't have all the experience.

By saying, 'A person in full consciousness of Me', Krishna is indicating here that the only time you can have full consciousness is by becoming Krishna conscious because Krishna is the full thing. Therefore Vyasadeva and Lord Brahma also, are saying, *janmady asya yatah*, that from which everything emanates, means the full thing. The whole science of Vedic knowledge is to study that full thing. That is called the absolute truth.

What is the meaning of absolute? Absolute means the full thing. There can't be anything outside of absolute. That's why people say, 'I'm absolutely sure'. 'I'm absolutely sure I saw that person before'. Although, in actuality, that is not the proper use of absolute. That is a wrong idea because, in the material - there is nothing absolute. Everything is relative. Everything is relating to our senses and sense objects. And the deficiency of those senses constitutes the deficiency of knowledge. If you have imperfect instruments, you have an imperfect result. You can't have imperfect instruments and have a perfect result. The body itself is imperfect; the result of our being here in this body is also imperfect. We have imperfect happiness, imperfect knowledge, imperfect existence, and we also have imperfect strength. We are always requiring help from outside.

So people think if we all get together, then collectively we can become perfect. Therefore you have social philosophies, materialism, capitalism, socialism, communism, altruism. All the little creatures get together and say, 'Okay, I don't have the perfect picture or the perfect solution, but if we all get together and do the same thing then we can collectively achieve perfection'. Perfection may come in the form of living in what they call a perfect society. This has always been the great search of life. We see that if we study the big Greek philosophers like Plato and Aristotle. If you study the philosophy of Plato's *Republic,* all of these great philosophers are trying to find the perfect solution to the problems the conditioned souls face in the material world.

This constant search is going on since time immemorial. And it'll go on until the end of doomsday. There will always be searching because we're very tiny. We're very inadequate. We require adequacy. We require some help from outside. That may come in the form of philosophy. It may come in the form of culture, education or social systems. Whatever it comes in, the idea is to find fullness, completeness and absolute perfection.

Krishna is saying that He is the only benefactor. Now that is a very difficult thing to comprehend. Because we then think that, 'I will be deprived. If He becomes the only benefactor, where is my benefit?' That's why the idea of God is always a very difficult thing for the conditioned soul to accept. Because if God is benefiting, what's the benefit for me? Therefore in every religion, the idea is you go to heaven, there must be a reward. You give money in charity, help the poor, dig wells in the villages and at the end, you go floating up to heaven. And in heaven, you have these beautiful gardens with beautiful damsels, beautiful music you can dance to, and nice liquor.

In every religion the idea is that let God benefit, but we have great difficulty to let God benefit. We don't want God to benefit. Why should He benefit? But if He does benefit, make sure I get something back. As it says in the *Bhagavatam, sai vai pumsam paro dharmo yato bhaktir adhoksaje ahaituky apratihata yayatma suprasidati.* This *Bhagavat Purana* is teaching about the highest perfection of religion or the highest *dharma. Paro dharmo* is that by which one obtains to transcendental loving service unto the Glorious Lord. That is considered by the *Bhagavatam* to be the highest level of perfection. The Supreme Lord should completely benefit from one's activities. And then it says *ahaituky apratihata,* there should be no motivation or interruption. Now to take away motivation from any living creature is very difficult because for billions of lifetimes we have been motivated. There is always this underlying principle of benefiting from a situation. We want to benefit and therefore in most religions, this idea of *ahaituky apratihata* is very difficult to comprehend. Here the word being used is *shantim.* What is the meaning of *shantim?* Relief from all material pangs.

Krishna is saying, 'Recognize Me as the supreme benefactor of sacrifices', *yajna tapasam.* The material world means sacrifice and austerity. As soon as you come here, you have to sacrifice. You have to suffer. What is the meaning of sacrifice? Sacrifice means voluntary suffering. Suppose I give you five hundred pounds, you're happy and I'm suffering from the loss. Sometimes a man gives a nice present to his wife. He likes that the wife is very happy, she says, 'Oh you shouldn't have bought me such a thing my darling!' And he's thinking, 'Yes, you're right, it cost me so much money'. Prabhupada said 'the friendly thief'. If someone comes and picks your pocket you become angry and hit them on the head or call the police. But if your wife takes your wallet and empties it, you say, 'Oh, my wife is so nice! How she emptied my wallet! I'll go and fill it up again, so she can empty it again tomorrow'. The children also come, 'Daddy give me this. Mummy give me that.' So they are the benefactor. Of what? Austerity, *yajna*, *tapasya*. Everything is *tapa*, in the sense that if you want to eat, you have to get the food. If you want the food, at least you have to grow it or you have to buy it. You must sacrifice something for that pleasure. Your pleasure is only coming because of some sacrifice. That is the law of *karma*. For every action, there is an equal and opposite reaction. In order to gain, we have to give. If you want a nice salary at the end of the week, you have to get up at eight o'clock, go to work and clock in at nine o'clock, 'Good morning boss, I'm here',

'Oh, you've come on time? Very good'.

The next day, he looks at his watch, 'Five minutes late! Don't be late tomorrow!',

'I'm sorry sir. I won't be late anymore. Please don't sack me'.

So we become like a dog, wagging our tail. What is the meaning of the dog? He takes shelter of some master. We are always actually performing different types of sacrifice, *yajna*, but because they're related to our body, we don't mind. If we work very hard we can have a nice car, a nice family and a nice suit to wear. We can have a nice bank account with Barclays or NatWest and look at all the noughts that we have. 'Yesterday it was five hundred, today it is six hundred'. We become very happy.

We want that we should benefit, but Krishna is saying, 'I am the only benefactor'. So what does that make us? It makes us thieves. Just like if you are working with a bank, the bank is the only benefactor of your work, you're not supposed to benefit. It's not that every time someone deposits ten thousand pounds, it goes your wallet. If you work for a bank and someone deposited ten million into the account, if you take even one ten pence, you could be thrown out. You can say, 'Look it was only ten pence. He gave me ten million. What are you complaining about, people? You're fanatics.' You can't say, 'I've been here for ten years collecting billions on your behalf. So what if I stole a few hundred? What is the problem?' No, you are a thief because the only benefactor is the bank.

Krishna is saying the same thing, 'I am the only benefactor'. This is very strong. That means despite all of the demigods, all of the patriarchs, all of the kings, all of the controllers on every level from the highest to the lowest of these planets in the universe, Krishna is the only benefactor. No other avatar, no other incarnation has spoken like this, in the history of any culture. There is no person. If you study Christianity, Greek philosophy, any philosophy you study, you will not find any individual who says, 'I'm the only benefactor in the whole creation'. Krishna is saying that every single thing within this universe is for His pleasure.

We're always trying to measure. I'm trying to measure myself against what? I'm measuring how good-looking I am with a mirror. What is a mirror? For measuring. That's why as you get older you don't look at it so much. There's not so much to measure. I want to measure how rich I am. I look at other people and the next-door neighbour has a better car than me. Have they got more money than me? We're constantly measuring, measuring to see what quantity we've got in this world. That's why one has to understand God. Without understanding God, there's no question of understanding oneself or the material energy. It's not possible unless you understand the creator, the sustainer and the destroyer of this energy. That is the meaning of Krishna consciousness. To understand how God is. Every single planet you see in the sky, Krishna is the Lord of that planet. So then He says *suhrdam sarva bhutanam*, He is the well-wisher of all living entities. People don't understand that. They mostly understand God to be the controller. 'Oh! Allah is coming. He will destroy all of these *kafirs*. He will kill them all!' They don't know *suhrdam sarva bhutanam*, Krishna is the well-wisher of all living entities because He loves everyone. We don't have any love for God but He has unlimited love for us. The benefit that we are gaining is on account of His desire. Everyone wants to benefit. We need food. We need air. We need light. We need so many things. So we are taking benefit. We are taking benefit from everywhere because we require benefit. That's why the government has the welfare benefits system because everyone requires benefit. You may be invalid or have medical needs, so the government is there to provide. You don't expect the next-door neighbour to provide you healthcare. It's not that you're expecting your neighbour should give your health care and provide you with free meals on wheels.

You can go to the government because the government is very great. If you go to a country where the government is not so great, you won't get anything. We see that when the country is great then there's great benefit. When God is great, then there is a great benefit to everyone. That's why if you study, you'll find no one is going hungry. All the animals have big bellies. In Africa, there are hundreds and thousands of elephants and you won't find one skinny elephant. I've never seen it. Have you ever seen a picture of a skinny elephant? The elephant needs hundreds of kilos of food every day. How many kilos are you consuming? Maybe two kilos worth. He's taking a hundred every day. Even the birds are flying. You don't find skinny birds. The birds also look nice. Big fat birds. You never see skinny crows crying because they didn't have a good dinner. As soon as they wake up, food is there.

So Krishna is providing because He's the well-wisher of everyone. He is providing everything for everyone. But because in the material world, we have this independent tendency, we are the masters of our suffering and our enjoyment. As Prabhupada used to say, 'Man proposes, God disposes'. Man is proposing what he wants by his activities. If I am acting in a sinful way, I will get a sinful reaction. If I am acting in a horrible way, I will get a horrible reaction. If I'm acting in a good way, I will get a good reaction.

If you go to the sweet shop and you can only spend ten pence and someone else spends a hundred pounds, the person behind the counter should not be blamed for giving that person more sweets than you. The person is giving according to your spending power. In the material world, you come here and if you are misusing your money, your energy, then you will become poor. And if you're using it properly you can increase it. Therefore, this word *suhrdam* is very important. Krishna says, 'I am the benefactor and well-wisher of all living entities'. One who accepts Krishna in this light, then he becomes *shanti*, full of freedom from the material pangs.

People want to know how to become free from the pangs of material life, but they don't know what the formula is. Your body requires food. You can decide, 'I'm very intelligent, I can put the food in my ear because this mouth is not able to take quickly enough', then you will not benefit because you don't know the correct method. The benefit is going to the stomach and when the stomach gets the benefit, it distributes to the rest of the body.

om purnam adah purnam idam purnat purnam udacyate
purnasya purnam adayah purnam evavasisyate
The Personality of Godhead is perfect and complete, and because He is completely perfect, all emanations from Him, are perfectly all equipped as complete wholes. (Isopanisad)

So all of these emanations that we have in this creation are all perfect and complete. This planet has the perfect facility to sustain the life of all the living creatures on this planet. You came here. Before Yorkshire, where did you come from Tom? You don't know, do you? Were you outside in a spaceship? You landed here in Yorkshire and everything was there immediately. The breast milk from the mother was there to give your tummy nice milk and to give your bones calcium, to give you proper nourishment. The mother is nourishing you, and you have taken shelter of your mother when you're born. And she has everything there. Similarly, this planet has everything to sustain you. From the moment you arrive in this world, to the moment you leave this world. Everything is completely arranged by the Supreme Personality of Godhead. You didn't bring anything with you. Nobody comes into this world with any extra arrangement. And whilst you're on this planet, you will not add anything to it. And when you leave you will not take anything away. There's no human being that adds anything to God's creation. There's no human being that brings anything into this creation, and there's no human being that takes anything out. But while we're here, we utilize everything. We're very expert at manipulating, exploiting and cheating. We are trying to keep everything in our possession. We make a big fancy juggling act, to make it appear that we are supplying. These big supermarkets are unable to create even one grain of rice from scratch. They're all thieves. They are very expert in stealing God's creation. Putting it on the shelves, and then charging you money. All of the chemical scientists in the world may be able to mess around with DNA or genetic engineering but they can't create it. No company has been producing one single thing which is not already there.

We can understand that Krishna has made a perfect arrangement for us. But the only thing that He's asking is to recognize Him. He's only asking one thing in this verse, that we recognize Him, nothing else. He's not asking that we do anything extra, except recognize. Krishna consciousness is simply the process of recognizing God. That's all. We're not big philosophers. We're not big industrialists or technicians. *Vaisnava* simply means to recognize that Krishna is the supreme enjoyer, the supreme controller and the supreme friend. Prabhupada said if you recognize these three things your life is perfect. You don't have to be a big scholar or a big industrialist. You simply have to recognize three things: That Krishna is the supreme enjoyer, the supreme controller and the supreme friend. Then your stealing mentality will go. Your cheating mentality will go. All of these demonic mentalities will go. Therefore Krishna consciousness is the science of studying Krishna. That's all. And therefore what is that perfection? *Satatam kirtayanto mam*. Krishna says always chanting My glories. *Drdha vratah*, with great determination and faith, they worship Me with devotion. Krishna consciousness means, first of all, become acquainted with the science of Krishna and then surrender to Krishna completely.

10: ENGAGE IN ACTIVITIES CONDUCIVE TO THE SOUL

A SHORT TALK GIVEN TO STUDENTS IN ENGLAND

Bhagavad-gita 6. 5
'One must deliver himself with the help of his mind, and not degrade himself. The mind is the friend of the conditioned soul, and his enemy as well'.

The illusory energy has captured strategic points in the body. Just like when an enemy takes over a city, the first thing it does is capture strategic points, such as the radio station, the TV station or the airport. If you're going to win a battle, you have to capture the strategic points. If you're attacking a city, there's no good capturing the sweetshop. If you announce, 'I captured the tobacco shop and the newspaper shop', it won't be very impressive. You have to go to the centre of communication as communication is the thing which influences people. In some countries, you hear the radio saying, 'Long live the prime minister or president or long live the Queen'.

There is so much propaganda going on because that is what influences the people in a society and similarly, on the fundamental level of our experience there is also a lot of propaganda. That propaganda is coming from the mind. The mind's business is to drag the living entity, the soul down. The two businesses of the material energy are to cover over and to drag down. These are the two potencies of the illusory energy. If you attack someone, the first thing you do is cover their eyes and then drag them down. Once you've covered their eyes it's easy to drag them down because they can't see what's going on. They immediately become confused, frightened and bewildered. But if they can see, it's more difficult to drag them down because they may see something to grab a hold of.

Maya's first business is to cover one over with ignorance or *avidya. Vidya* means knowledge and *avidya* means ignorance. *Maya* steals away knowledge

95

from the living entity. Knowledge has an eternal relationship with the soul because our nature is to be full of knowledge. We cannot exist without knowledge. We search after it twenty-four hours a day. When we get up in the morning we immediately ask, 'Where is my toothbrush?', 'Where did I leave my sweater?' or 'Where is the light?' Sometimes if you're in a room you're unfamiliar with, the first thing you try to do is find the light. And if you don't know where the light switch is you feel like a real idiot. You may start looking around and you find out it's not in the room at all but it's outside. Then you become frustrated because.

From the moment we get up in the morning, we are always searching for things. By our very nature, we are always inspecting things. We want to bring everything into an inspection mode, to see what is favourable and what is unfavourable. Just like when food comes along you inspect it. Is there any curd *sabji* there? Are there any samosas today? And if it's just boiled parsnips, then you think, 'Oh, cheated again!' We are always looking for that which is conducive to our happiness. That's why everyone is looking around in the material world. We are looking for those things which are very tasty for ourselves. The boy is looking for a very tasty girl and the girl is looking for a very tasty boy. If he doesn't look good - if he has got cross-eyes and his nose is falling off, the girls don't look twice. So everybody is trying to look very tasty.

In the material world, everything is based upon *rasa*. *Rasa* means that thing which gives taste. Something which looks beautiful gives taste. If you look at an expensive car, you get the feeling that this is very nicely designed. If you look at a flower, a sunrise or a sunset, it's very pleasing, so you are getting a nice experience and a feeling that this is very pleasing to the senses. Whereas if you look at a dead body splattered all over the road, it's not very pleasing.

What we are looking for is perfection, but we are looking for it in an imperfect world. We have tried to find something perfect in the imperfect. The nature of *maya*, illusion, is that she actually covers over the knowledge of the living entity. This is called conditional life. We are put into different conditions. Everybody has a certain type of conditioning. Someone is conditioned by the fact that they were born in a particular country.

Just like in psychology, they always bring you back to your childhood to find out what experiences you had that made you like you are now. They may look at if you were brought up by a very dominant parent or a very cruel parent, then you may be psychologically disturbed. If you were brought up in a very poor country in a very neglectful way, then there will be other types of disturbances. These conditions are actually brought about on account of association with matter. We have nothing to do with these material conditions. The material conditions are a phantasmagoria, they only last temporarily.

We have gone through many different situations but now they're all simply a dream. It didn't have any significance. It's just a mental creation. In one sense we create so many different situations. We're thinking that I am a twenty-year-old. This is my mother. This is my father. This is my brother. This is my sister. I'm English, Irish, French, Spanish or Portuguese. Someone else is thinking I'm a porcupine or a vegetable or a fruit.

The soul has nothing to do with the mind or the body. At night we sleep, but our mind is still creating so many things. Sometimes we're being attacked by a tiger. Sometimes we're running after money. Sometimes we are falling in love. Sometimes we are jumping off a mountain or flying in the sky. So many things go through the mind but in actuality, the body is lying there doing nothing. The mind is the constant companion of the living entity.

The *Bhagavad-gita* explains there is the gross and the subtle body. The subtle body is the mind, the intelligence and false ego. We can see practically that from the mind one can become degraded or elevated. It's not difficult to become degraded. You can go take intoxication, hang out with the wrong sort of people, and gradually become degraded. We can also become elevated by the mind, but it depends upon association.

We have to choose the type of association we want. If we want to associate with the mundane, with the temporary world and if we want to come under the clutches of *maya,* illusion - then we make that choice. We have a choice. We cannot blame God for our predicament. The *Bhagavad-gita* explains that we are in our condition because of our own fault. The idea that God creates catastrophe is wrong, He doesn't. Actually, God only allows catastrophe to happen because that's what we're due. It is created by your *karma*.

The government doesn't arrange the prison because people want to go to prison. Nobody wants a holiday in prison. The prison is there because of the rebellious activities of a small number of citizens. If the citizens refuse to acknowledge the laws of the state, they become criminals and have to be subjected to punishment. The idea of the punishment is actually to reform. You don't put people in prison because you want them to be in prison but to reform their character and nature. The human form of life is the opportunity to reform oneself. If you don't then you will have to go down again into the cycle of repeated birth and death in various types of species. You will be dragged there by the mind.

The mind in association with the modes of material nature creates 8,400,000 different types of bodies. Sometimes you see people going into a shop buying different types of clothes. If you want to be a lumberjack, you buy lumberjack clothes. If you want to be a builder on a building site, you buy builders' clothes. If you want to go to the disco and show off, you buy those clothes. If you want to be a judge, you buy those clothes. If you want to be an actor at the theatre, you buy those clothes. If you want to go swimming on the beach, you buy those clothes. The clothes are provided according to the desire. It's not that they created the people to fit the clothes.

The gross comes from the subtle. In other words, the subtle creates the gross. And then the gross dictates to the subtle. This is what we call the cycle of *samsara* - the interaction between subtle and gross energy. Just like starting from just the subtle, an idea, we create a pub. So the subtle manifests the gross. Then people go to the pub and there's disco music, alcohol, some meat to eat, some intoxication and smoking. Once people go into the pub, they become a victim of the gross. The subtle element, the mind is thinking, 'I better go get another drink, I better have another smoke, I better eat some meat. I better go and chat that girl up and see if she's ever met such a handsome guy as me before. I'll tell her how lucky she is to be in the same bar as a guy like me'. So the gross ends up controlling the subtle. We end up getting dictated to by our mind and senses. This is the way the subtle is being dictated by the circumstances.

As soon as you implicate yourself with that process, you get subjected to *karma*. The action causes a reaction and the reaction causes more action. You go after a beautiful girl, talk to her and then she says, 'Let's go', and you have dinner at a restaurant and spend all of your hard-earned money and then she buzzes off, 'Thanks for the meal! I have to go now'. And then the guy is in the middle of the road stranded, with all of his money gone, feeling disappointed that he was thinking he would get some further pleasures.

That's the material world. We are here for a very short duration of time but we are still concocting so many different dreams. We're going to do this and we're going to do that. 'Things are going to get better. Things are looking good now, I just got a pay rise. I just got a date.' Gradually we see that all of these phantasmagorias gradually disappear. And all we are left with is old age, bronchitis, arthritis or senile dementia. After all of that running around, endeavouring, bringing up a family and everything - all we get left with is some senile dementia. That's the result. Intelligence means to at least learn from others' mistakes. If you can't even learn from your own mistakes, look at others.

The best way to develop intelligence is by hearing. One can immediately be picked up from this mundane world simply by hearing knowledge from the transcendental plane. This transcendental sound is descending from the highest plane, beyond the interaction of matter and time. Beyond past, present and future. This transcendental knowledge is coming from another plane, where there is no presence of birth, old age, disease and death. That plane is called *Vaikuntha*: the place where there are no anxieties. That is the actual plane upon which the soul exists in its eternality. On that plane there is no actual hostility.

Why is there no hostility? Because the natural function of the soul is to live in an environment conducive to his existence. We're always looking for a conducive environment because we belong in one. At the moment we are like fishes out of water. We actually belong in a conducive and a conscious environment. The spiritual world is fully conscious and therefore everything reciprocates completely and perfectly. In the material world, things do not reciprocate because they are inert, they're unconscious.

If you go into a room and someone goes in before you and slam the door in your face, you become very annoyed. 'How rude! How unconscious of that person to do that!' So you see that when people are not conscious of you, it becomes a disturbance. Matter is not conscious of you. It is an inert substance that you are trying to manipulate but matter does not actually reciprocate with you, despite your efforts. This is called the struggle for existence. We want everything to reciprocate with our desires but because nothing does, we are full of anxiety. We desire to be happy and we find that practically speaking there is very little happiness in the material world, and the main forms of happiness in the material world come from reciprocation, *rasa*.

We are animate living entities in an inanimate environment. The nature of animation is that it is personal. Consciousness means animation. It has some sort of reciprocation, desires and feelings. The soul is animate but at the moment it is mixed up with an inanimate substance and this is causing many disturbances because we want to bring the energy under a certain degree of subjugation, so it will reciprocate with us. The reason we try to control matter is so it reciprocates with us.

Our attempt to control is a great struggle as the material energy is always more powerful than us. Krishna explains in the *Bhagavad-gita* that *mama maya duratyaya*, you can never control the material energy, rather you are always controlled by it. And therefore by nature, you are a servant. But instead of serving our mind and our material desires, we should try to serve the controller of this material world. That is Krishna.

If speculation was able to bring happiness then everyone would be very happy, as everyone spends their time speculating. If speculation was going to bring happiness, the whole world would be rolling around in ecstasy. People spend their whole life speculating and it brings them nothing. It doesn't bring them any tangible happiness but rather it gives them anxiety. We are tiny speculators and we have a very tiny ability to control the material energy.

We see that instead of finding solutions to our problems, we actually increase the problems because the process is dysfunctional. It's wrong. Therefore we have to hear. We have to submit ourselves to higher sound. Because that sound - if it is coming from the pure plane - can give us perfect truth. If the knowledge is perfect, it's coming from a perfectly pure source, that knowledge can free us from illusion.

It is an audacity to think that we can control our mind. We are trying to control material nature but we cannot even control our own mind. This is arrogance on the part of the living entity. The living entity is controlled by earth, water, fire, air and ether. Just like your body is made up of those elements, but you're spending your own life serving that body.

From the moment you are born until you die, you spend your whole life serving the body. And what does the body do? It simply decays. After all of that service you've given it: all of that food, all of that makeup you put on it, all of that cleaning it and pampering it - it just starts to rot, right in front of you. It's not very grateful, is it? It just decays right there, in front of your very eyes and as it decays it starts to smell and decay more and then finally it dwindles. And all you're left with is a few bones and a bit of skin hanging on. That's the reality.

You are being controlled by this body. You are not the controller. You're the servant of the body. You have taken up the service of earth, water, fire, air and ether. You have taken up service of your mind and false ego but these things will never bring you pleasure or satisfaction. They'll only bring you hostility and anxiety.

Krishna consciousness means to understand that I should use my mind to serve Krishna. I should use this body, this bag of skin and bone to serve Krishna. I must use my intelligence to serve Krishna. I must use the material energy to serve Krishna. I must use everything for His satisfaction. Why? Because He is the controller, He is the creator, He is the enjoyer.

The tendency we have is we want to make everything serve us, but we are being cheated. Nothing will serve us. Things will simply inflict some misery upon us. And this is the grace of Krishna. This is the mercy of Krishna. Don't think that your suffering is something negative. It is very positive. It is there to warn you, don't go down this road.

Like if you're going down a very dark road and you know that there are tigers, lions and other jungle animals around, then you don't roam down there, do you? You become very introspective. Should I go down there? I heard there are dangerous snakes there. I may get bitten by a tarantula or I may get attacked by a wild lion. So the material world is like that. The hostility of the material world is to make you think. 'Should I go down this path? Should I go there?' Look what is waiting down there: old age, disease, death and so many negative things. The intelligent person can understand, 'I should not follow this path, I should not go down this road. But rather I should take the other road'. I should elevate my consciousness to go back home back to Godhead by chanting:

Hare Krishna Hare Krishna
Krishna Krishna Hare Hare
Hare Rama Hare Rama
Rama Rama Hare Hare

Krishna says, 'For him who has conquered the mind, the mind is the best of friends, but for one who has failed to do so, his mind is the greatest enemy' We can conquer the mind when we surrender the mind to Krishna. As soon as you surrender your mind to Krishna, then it becomes your greatest friend. As soon as you try to dominate matter, to manipulate matter, to utilize matter, then your mind becomes the worst enemy.

There's no greater suffering than the mind. Any disease that you get in this world is nothing compared to the misery of the mind. That's because the mind is the key factor in our experiences. And therefore Krishna inflicts the maximum displeasure from the mind, so that you do not take shelter of that mind. That's His causeless mercy. If you take shelter of the mind then you may again be degraded down into various species. Krishna makes your mind the most unfriendly element. So that you can understand, I should not befriend this person. Just like if you're with a very nasty person, you don't want to be with him.

This material world is a nasty place. But we're thinking somehow or other, we can change it. As Srila Bhaktisiddhanta Sarasvati Thakura used to say, 'This material world is no place for a gentleman'. It is hostile to our real interest. And therefore we should not try to associate with it. The best thing to do with the mind is to engage it in Krishna's service. Don't try to associate with it. It's not you. Just like you don't try to associate with your skin or your body because it's not you. You have to move on to another level where you don't associate with the mind. Our trouble is that we want to absorb ourselves in the mind. And then we wonder why we're suffering. The mind has to be active. It's either elevating or degrading you. There's no real in-between.

Prabhupada says: *The mind must be so trained that it can deliver the conditioned soul from the mire of nescience. In material existence one is subjected to the influence of the mind and the senses. In fact, the pure soul is entangled in the material world because the mind is involved with the false ego, which desires to Lord it over material nature.*
Therefore, the mind should be trained so that it will not be attracted by the glitter of material nature, and in this way the conditioned soul may be saved. One should not degrade oneself by attraction to sense objects. The more one is attracted by sense objects, the more one becomes entangled in material existence. The best way to disentangle oneself is to always engage the mind in Krishna consciousness.

The only way that the mind can be free from material attraction is by tasting superior attraction and the most superior attraction is Krishna. If one does not become attracted to Krishna, then one cannot be saved. The material energy is so powerful that if you're not attracted to Krishna then you will become attracted to the material world. Therefore if one can become attracted to Krishna then one can be saved from the degradation of mind.

11: AVOID STEREOTYPED LIFE

A TALK TO BHAKTI YOGA STUDENTS
AT ISKCON BIRMINGHAM, UK - 10 NOVEMBER 1997

Sometimes people accuse us spiritualists, that we are neglecting the primary necessities of life. What are the primary necessities of life? Looking after the bodily needs: eating, sleeping, enjoying, having a sex life and fearing. People think that without these things one will surely die and will not be able to exist. People feel that these activities of the material world are very much necessary and very much required. They are obsessed with the bodily concept of life. They feel that maintenance of the body is the all in all of existence and that there is no higher principle than looking after your body. They think that the body itself is the primary importance of life.

This ideology is often compared to that of a *mudha,* a donkey. If you study the donkey, he is a very wonderful character because he has a gross stupid-looking body with big genitals and his primary concern is the opposite sex. When he approaches a female, sometimes they kick him in the face with both legs and you hear a crack. He thinks his voice is very sweet and poetic but this *hee-haw* sound is a very loud and obnoxious noise to others, and therefore sometimes people give him a beating. The poor donkey has to work very hard just for some grass. He carries very heavy loads on his back because no one cares a damn about the donkey. They use them for carrying things up mountainsides. In India on building sites, they load them up with a huge amount of bricks on their back. In Cairo, I saw people kick them hard. And at the end of the day all they get is a little grass because if you don't give them some grass, they'll die. They put a little sack under his mouth and whilst he's eating his grass he's thinking, 'Everything is fine, everything is very nice, look at this nice grass that I've got to eat!'

This is the nature of this world. Even though the living entity is in a very pathetic situation, he is engaged in these stereotyped worldly affairs. Everyone is doing the same thing. The only difference between what we and

105

the donkey are doing, is that we are just doing it in a more polished way. We are having a little better sex life, a little better eating and a little better sleeping. But at the same time, we have much more anxiety than a donkey. You don't find a mental home for a disturbed donkey, do you? I haven't seen a mentally disturbed donkey but I've seen many mentally disturbed humans because the human being is full of anxieties. These anxieties exist because the human is so arrogant and proud that he thinks he's the controller, even though he's actually controlling nothing. He can't even control his own sleeping patterns.

We are controlled by our bodily necessities. We have to eat – as soon as the lunch bell rings, we are down there and with a moist tongue. As soon as we see a pretty girl, we are immediately disturbed, 'Oh, here is some nice sex life'. As soon as there is a nice opportunity for sleeping, everyone is very eager to have a snooze. And we are full of anxieties all the time. 'I am in control. I am the big shot around here. I have to worry about everything, and without me, the whole universe will collapse. The economy would collapse. The government would go out of business. This girl would be finished'.

These are the ways people think. Even though it sounds exaggerated everyone feels that, 'Things are going on because of me'. The whole egocentric conception of the mind is that all things are centred around me. That's why people love to have the news brought to them so that they can check everything out and inspect it. To make sure that things are going on according to their plan. So they like to keep up to date with what's going on, as if it's very important to them. What difference are they going to make if they read it or don't read it? It's still going to happen. They have to inspect it. They have to look to see, 'What did they do today? Oh, I don't agree with this. I don't agree with that!'

They have many opinions, but they are all useless because nature is created with very stringent and precise laws. Prabhupada said there are even laws for how many times you blink in a day. There are demigods in charge of the blinking of your eye. There are demigods in charge of the water, the sun and the moon. Everything is controlled very finely and microscopically. Not like when we try to control something - we are thick-headed, absent-minded, stupid and pathetic.

That is not how Krishna's arrangement is going on. It is going on very precisely. Your body is a precise mechanism which is crafted to interact with another mechanism. Your body is created to interact with food. When you eat, many things in your body correspond to the eating of that food. How did they get there? How did they know you are going to put in certain types of foodstuffs? A lion is expertly created for eating meat, he's a meat-eating machine. There's no good feeding him grapes. His body is created for a certain function – his body is perfect for meat-eating. He doesn't need a cooker, he doesn't need a pan, and he doesn't need a menu. He doesn't need any recipes. He has beautiful claws that can rip apart a body in seconds, in minutes he can have it all ripped to shreds and his teeth can bite into big bones, even elephant bones with his very powerful jaws. Some lions can put your head in their mouth and just crack it like a nut. Especially when you have a small head. *Poof*! It would be the end of that! He could chew it up like eating candy.

An intelligent personality can understand. Are these activities related to me? That's a good question. Who are you? That is the most important question. *Athato brahma jjinasa.* Now is the time to find out. Am I just a being who is here to fulfil his animalistic nature of eating, sleeping, mating and defending? As long as you have a human body these things are connected with your consciousness. Naturally, by Krishna consciousness, these propensities for eating, sleeping, mating and defending and fearing become increasingly reduced. Fearing also is the idea that I might miss something.

'Here I am in the prime of my youth. I have a wonderful body. The girls are always looking at me. They can just about handle my handsome features and my wonderful abilities. They have yet to see my mastership over knowledge and qualities. I have to reveal to them my wonders. But should I miss that opportunity? Look at what I will be missing. The world might not be able to see the unlimited display that I am capable of doing. The girls will not be able to have the wonderful pleasure of being in my company, having my strong arms around them to give them protection, to give them the shelter that they need'.

The foolish living entity thinks that somehow or other he has something to offer to the material world. And this anxiety is that, 'I must find myself, this cow of plenty, who can give me lots of nice sense gratification. And I can, of course, give her wonderful things that she has never had before. I am so wonderful that this link should be made as soon as possible'.

These anxieties and fears exist on so many different levels. That anxiety that this sense gratification may pass me by. If I become too absorbed in Krishna's service, these years are going by me. 'Before I was twenty-four and now I am thirty. Oh my goodness, all those ladies out there are going to be crying soon because I will be a little bit too old. They won't be so attracted to me'. So this fear is there. 'Oh no! I'm going to live to be ripe and old. What will I do in my old age? I won't have any little *kiddy widdies* to look after me, no wife to comfort me, no house to shelter me. I will simply be disregarded by everyone because of my old age and feebleness'.

All of these anxieties haunt the mind. But they are all *maya*. *Maya* means, 'that which is not'. This world is making me an ass because I am thinking, 'I am this body'. This useless combination of elements that have nothing to do with the Supreme Personality of Godhead. Would you offer Krishna some mucus? Would you offer Krishna some bile? Some bad stinky air? Some bones? What is it in your body that you can offer Krishna? Rather you have to constantly wash your body even to bring it into the temple. It's such a disgusting place to be in. What is it that you have got in your body that is of any use to Krishna? You can pull out a few veins. Do you think Krishna needs a few veins? There's nothing about your body that is of any use to anyone.

But there are millions of things in your mind that you think are useful to everyone. Millions and billions of things haunt your mind. 'Yes, I'm so useful. I am so important. I am so needed. I am so wonderful I can't even cope with it anymore!'

This is the nature of illusion, *maya*. She makes us feel that this tiny little stop-gap life of a few seconds is a long time. We don't know how long we will live. We have no jurisdiction over time. There are many people lying in graves right now, being eaten by worms, that thought they were going to be doing something this week. Look at our princess who just died. She is now starting to be eaten by maggots. That nice body that charmed the minds of so many men that saw her in the glossy magazines, now the little old maggots are going to have their feast. She thought she was going to be cruising down the highway with little old prince this and prince that, to wherever, to meet whomever. She thought so many things, and there are many people like her, lying in their little coffins. All of those places she planned to visit are still there and her big bank balance is still there, but she isn't there anymore.

That is the reality. We think we are going to live and we have faith in this world that these things are going to be very important, our future is very important. One must not neglect his future! The future could be very amazing, it could be wonderful! We could become anything! But in actuality, the future isn't ours. It doesn't belong to us, it belongs to Krishna. Krishna is the lord of time. Therefore, it is His future. Whatever He wants will happen. This paranoia of life is another transformation of the mind in association with material illusion. The mind is full of so much nonsense and garbage, but in reality, if you look at it - no man can claim the next second as his own. Not one person can claim he is going to live for one hour more.

The constant transmigration of the soul from one body to another is the cause of suffering in material existence but we want to prolong it. We want to sustain and protect the very thing which is causing our suffering - our attachment to the material world and our material body. That means we are materialists. We are not devotees. We are materialists as we are worried about material things. A devotee is worried about Krishna, whether He feels satisfied with my activities. Whether Krishna is pleased by what I am doing. Whether Krishna is pleased by my plan-making.

Look back on everything you have done until now. What part of it was significant? What part has given you any permanent good? Does it matter how many meals you ate or how many people you talked to or how many beds you lied on? All of these things we have done, we will do them over and over again. We are chewing the chewed. We are constantly chewing on the same old thing over and over again. Later on, we will look back and say, 'What was it that I did, that was of any significance?' Ask all of these people that have produced so many children and worked their hearts out. Ask them, 'Be honest, was it all worth it?' Very few of them can actually say the whole thing was worth it because all of those little *kiddy widdies* that they've brought up, they've all gone off and done their own thing, leaving their parents to get old and decrepit, and then when they get too old they'll stuff them in a home for the senile because they interfere with their sense gratification.

The material nature is very cruel to the foolish living entities. She does not tolerate their foolish activities, she is always constantly whipping them and smashing them so that somehow or other they may wake up and realise that these activities are all useless animalistic activities. They are no different than the cow, the hog or the dog - sniffing around, eating something, having a bit of sex and falling asleep. It's no different. We may do them in big houses but they're all the same bodily activities. They are related to the material world and they will not give any nectar to the soul because these activities are not related to Krishna.

Krishna consciousness means to *Krishna-ise* everything, to transform this energy into the service of Krishna. This energy should be used to glorify *Urukrama*, the Supreme Personality of Godhead who performs wonderful activities. Those activities of Krishna are beyond the stereotype affairs of this material world, beyond the beastly activities of matter. Krishna says *bhogaisvarya*, for those who are too much attached to material sense gratification the resolute determination for devotional service does not take place. There is a very fine line between being engaged in Krishna's service and being engaged in your material desires, your service, and devotional service is naturally a declaration of war on the material energy.

In the *Gurvastakam* prayers we sing every morning, it says *samsara,* which means this world of repeated cycle of birth. *Samsara dava* means that this world is like a great blazing forest fire. When a huge forest catches fire, the little drops of water that we throw on it don't have any effect. We may see a big forest fire so we try to put the fire out with this small bucket, you can just about carry it because it's so heavy anyway and by the time you get there you've spilt half of it and by the time you actually manage to throw it on the fire it doesn't even make an impression. It even looks like it increased it. It looks like it didn't have any effect at all. It is a pathetic endeavour to put out a forest fire. Even if the big fire engines come along, what can they do? Their engine and all of their tubing will all be melted because forest fire is a huge amount of heat. They even sometimes send helicopters over it but they don't work either. You have to see a forest fire to really understand it. Sometimes it destroys thousands of acres, so the only one single hope is a huge storm cloud will come.

At the end of this *yuga* is the devastation, where the universe gets burnt up by the fire of the sun and then these clouds wash away the whole universe. These clouds are compared to the shelter of the spiritual master and the *Srimad Bhagavatam*. They are compared to the shelter of the *guru*, the s*astra* (books) and *sadhus* (saintly persons) - these elements make the soothing shelter of the umbrella of Krishna consciousness. One who has taken shelter under this raincloud of Krishna consciousness can be protected from the fire of material life. So one has to take shelter.

Prabhupada says: *The raging forest fire can be extinguished only when there is a constant downpour of water from a cloud. The cloud is compared to the mercy of the spiritual master. By the grace of the spiritual master the cloud of the mercy of the personality of Godhead is brought in, and then only, when the rains of Krishna consciousness fall, can the fire of material existence be extinguished. In order to find freedom from the stereotyped conditional life of material existence, one has to take shelter of the lotus feet of the Lord, not in the manner in which the impersonalists indulge, but in devotional service, chanting and hearing of the activities of the Lord.*

Chanting and hearing are very important. It's not a stereotyped reading of a book, rather it's meditation on the transcendental pastimes and form of Krishna. One must become convinced about Krishna, otherwise this chanting and hearing will not take place. Why is it people are so convinced about the material world? Because they have conviction in material life. They have faith that if they have a nice house, family, bank balance and so many things, that they will be happy. They have faith in it.

Similarly, we must have the same faith in Krishna. Otherwise, we will not engage in the activities of Krishna consciousness. Why is it that certain people don't become very enthusiastic about activities in the material world? Because they lose faith. Similarly, why is it that certain devotees are not very enthusiastic in Krishna consciousness? Because they lose faith. Everything hinges on faith. If you don't have faith in Krishna, then you cannot perform devotional service. The first thing is *sraddha*, faith. Without the required faith, there will be no determination. People act according to gain. Naturally, we all act to gain something. So if we don't think there's anything to be gained, we won't do anything to gain it.

12: ENJOYMENT MEANS TWO

A TALK GIVEN IN
ISKCON BIRMINGHAM, UK - 12 NOVEMBER 1997

Srimad Bhagavatam 3.21.19
*"My dear Lord, You alone create the universes. O Personality of
Godhead, desiring to create these universes, You create them,
maintain them and again wind them up by Your own energies,
which are under the control of Your second energy, called
yogamaya, just as a spider creates a cobweb by its own energy
and again winds it up."*

Purport
*In this verse two important words nullify the impersonalist
theory that everything is God. Here Kardama says, "O Personality
of Godhead, You are alone, but You have various energies." The
example of the spider is very significant also. The spider is an
individual living entity, and by its energy it creates a cobweb and
plays on it, and whenever it likes it winds up the cobweb, thus
ending the play. When the cobweb is manufactured by the saliva
of the spider, the spider does not become impersonal. Similarly,
the creation and manifestation of the material or spiritual energy
does not render the creator impersonal. Here the very prayer
suggests that God is sentient and can hear the prayers and fulfil
the desires of the devotee. Therefore, He is sac-cid-ananda-
vigraha [Bs. 5.1], the form of bliss, knowledge and eternity.*

According to Vedic philosophy, *eko bahunam*, there is originally one and that
one becomes many. This is the philosophy of *acintya bhedabheda tattva,* the
Supreme Personality of Godhead is one but that same one has become many.
This is a very important understanding of God. God's spiritual energy is all-
pervading, therefore God is all-pervading. We are not all-pervading but we

are localized within this body, therefore we are limited. We have a local and a very limited jurisdiction.

Our individuality is repulsive in many ways because we are very tiny. So the idea that God would be localized is repulsive to the impersonalists because they say that would make Him very limited. This is their psychology. This is their philosophy. They naturally think that the idea that God could be localized must put some limitation on God. So, therefore, they are much more attracted to the idea that God should be all-pervasive energy or that God should be so spread out that He is indescribable, unknowable, unthinkable, unspeakable and untouchable. This is refuted in the Vedic literature because although the Supreme Lord is one, He has become many because those are the sporting activities of God.

Although we are one person, in our individuality we like to have different roles. Sometimes we like to be the boss and we like to control people and their situations. Sometimes we want to be the lover, the *casanova*. Sometimes we want to be a great football player, a tennis player or a swimmer. Sometimes we want to be a big scientist or a mathematician or a philosopher. Sometimes we want to be a cook. But because we are tiny, each activity we perform is also tiny. We may be able to cook a few meals but can we cook for the whole universe? We may be able to control a few little people but can we control billions of universes? We may be able to love one woman or a few women but can we love millions at the same time? So that is the difference between us and God.

The idea that God is simultaneously one and retains His individuality is very difficult for people to grasp because it indicates some sort of localized limitation. As soon as one is localized, then the idea is how can it then be all-pervasive? It's contradictory to say that something is localized and at the same time it's everywhere.

Therefore, it says in the *Isopanisad*:

tad ejati tan naijati
tad dure tad v antike
tad antar asya sarvasya
tad u sarvasyasya bahyatah

The Supreme Lord walks and does not walk. He is far away, but He is very near as well. He is within everything, and yet He is outside of everything. (Isopanisad Text 5)

These are all 'contradictions'. These are all very difficult things to understand. Contradiction has to exist in God. It can't exist in us because we are under laws and to contradict the laws is not within our scope. If you opened your mouth and the sun was inside of your mouth, that would be pretty unusual, isn't it? But when Krishna opens His mouth, billions and trillions of universes are in His mouth. Therefore, you can understand that He is no ordinary person. And therefore he is called *saktiman*. Here the word is used *sva saktibhih*, 'by His own energy'. The example is used that a spider is in one place but at the same time, he extends his energy in the form of a web. So that anyone who enters into his energy, the web, gets entangled. Many little flies like to fly around, but if they come anywhere near the web they immediately become entangled in it.

Like it says here, the Lord had a desire to create because He's a person. You all have a desire to create but most of us just create a mess, a disturbance. The desire to create is in all of us. But we're not very good creators. Our creations appear to be very wonderful, but they are pretty useless. They are just tiny imitations of nature. Most creations are imitations of nature. Just like the aeroplane comes from the bird.

Krishna *says bija aham*, 'I am the seed'. This principle of the seed has to be understood because God is there in seed form. That's why all these scientists are very interested in seeds. By manipulation, they try to change the product. They can't create the seeds but they can only manipulate the seeds. Krishna is so powerful that He can create so many wonderful seeds. The universes are all emanating from the pores of His body.

In this verse, two important words nullify the impersonalist theory that everything is God. Here Kardama says, "O Personality of Godhead, You are alone, but You have various energies". (Srimad Bhagavatam 3.21.19 Purport)

It is very important to understand how the energies work, but one must also understand who the energetic is. One must understand the difference between the energy and the energetic. A man may create a car but that doesn't mean that the car is the man. The man and the car are two different things. If you study a car, does that mean you'll know the man? No. You may get an idea that, 'If he can create a car, this man must be pretty intelligent'. Unfortunately, when people study nature they think they know God. That is their stupidity. By studying nature how can you know God? If you don't know what God is, you won't know what His nature is. Just like if you pass stool in the toilet bowl, 'Oh, there's Andrew in the toilet bowl', and it's true, that's you because you left it there didn't you? It came out of you, it's part of you. Everything in your body is part of you but that doesn't mean that if someone studied the stool in the toilet bowl, then they've found you. If you study material energy and you think that, 'I found God because I studied the material energy', then you are a fool, *mudha*.

Krishna says, a*vajananti mam mudha*, 'The fools and rascals do not understand why I come to this material world, they do not understand My appearance in the material world'. Why? Because they think, 'Krishna has also taken a material body. He's also become like me'. Therefore they have foolish conceptions. Without understanding God, you cannot understand how His energy is working. Until you understand the person, how can you understand the energy of the person?

If you want to understand me, how are you going to do it? There are so many things you don't know. You can speculate, but the only way you can know about me is by hearing, isn't it? You can speculate, 'Maybe this, perhaps that'.

But you don't know anything because everyone has aspects of their lives that you don't know. Therefore this speculative process is very imperfect because if you can imagine, you cannot even know an individual until they reveal themself. How do you get to know someone? They have to reveal themselves to you.

'Hey, do you know I'm a psychopathic murderer?'
'No, you're not!'
'You don't know if I am or not. You have no proof that I'm not a psychopathic murderer.'
You may say, 'Well you don't look like one.'

Then he might say, 'Yes, but a lot of people who are don't look like one'.

Therefore, you can understand that is the whole business of the material world. People reveal things about themselves. 'Hey, Prabhu! I've got a few problems'. You can understand things much better by hearing, as that person will reveal things to you. You have to wait and develop an understanding by hearing. Just like if a boy meets a girl they have to reveal themselves to each other. It's very logical and very simple. The girl has to tell the boy, 'By the way, did you know I've got this or that'. So the boy may ascertain so many things but only when he's heard from the girl he will ascertain whether he wants to continue. Just like if a boy meets a girl and then the girl says, 'I can't have children'. Suddenly that boy is going to start thinking, 'Do I want to marry this girl if she can't even have children?' Even though he may be very attracted to her, he has to hear certain details from her which are very important to the relationship.

In the same way, everybody wants a relationship with God, but they don't want to hear from Him. We are individuals and we know that to have a relationship with each other, it's essential to hear from each other. Otherwise, we don't know what we are getting involved in. The person could be a complete cuckoo. Looking is not very important. The important thing is hearing from each other. The boy and the girl revealing themselves to each other is a very important part of the relationship.

Because when they start saying things like,
'By the way, did you know I murdered six people?'
And the girl is thinking inside, 'My goodness'.
'But it's alright, I won't murder you! I murdered six other women. I get a bit excited and sometimes I chop their heads off, I bury them underneath the patio!'
That girl's going to be gone as fast as she can! That is the revelation.

Even to understand tiny insignificant creatures, we need to hear. We need to read about what cockroaches are. When we see a fox, we need to read about the fox to know what it is. We need to read about things. It's no good just looking at something. If you are in Africa and you see a big spider, you may be thinking, 'Does it bite? Is it poisonous? Will it catch me? What will it do to me?' Or if you see a snake, you don't know what it is until you hear. And then the scientist says, 'If this snake bites you, you will have two minutes to live, so you better keep well away from that snake'. Whereas if he said the snake was harmless you wouldn't be so fearful. So your reaction is upon hearing about that particular thing. Everything has to be heard about in order to be understood. We even have to hear about the simplest things to understand them. It's no good speculating.

Similarly, what to speak of the Supreme Personality of Godhead. One has to hear about Him. We cannot understand God by speculation and imagination. So Krishna is explaining His transcendental nature through His devotee Kardama Muni, saying He is like a spider. The spider is in one place but at the same time spreads his energies everywhere.

If you look at the spider it's very wonderful because he just stays in one place, has a snooze and as soon as anyone touches his web, the vibration of the web is connected with his body. So immediately, he awakens and sees some prey has come and he attacks it very quickly. A spider can throw the web into the wind quite far and stick onto something with it. And then he uses that to make a cobweb. This is all mystical. This is called *acintya sakti*, inconceivable. Even the little spider is bewildering to us. The scientist is still trying to study where they get the material coming out of their body from. In relative terms to the spider's size, if you took the same fibre, it's ten times stronger than steel. That's incredibly hard stuff. So you can imagine what the poor old fly feels when he gets trapped in it. It's like getting caught up in a huge net of steel. So this spider can produce all of that. How does the spider do it?

If we can't even understand a little garden spider, what hope have we got of understanding God by our speculation? We haven't got a snowball's chance in hell. We haven't got a hope in hell of finding out what God is. Therefore, these tiny little concoctions that come out of the mind of man are simply a useless waste of time. They think that because God is great, therefore He's so great He can't be a person. That's absolutely ridiculous because to say that God can't be a person is a total limitation on God. God can be whatever He likes. That is the meaning of God, He is completely independent. Without independence how can He be God? Is He dependent on your descriptions? Is He dependent on the laws of nature? Is He under any jurisdiction? If God is not under any jurisdiction or any conditions, then He can do whatever He likes, whenever He likes. But people can't understand this simple thing that when God becomes a boar and He comes out of the nose of Lord Brahma. We think these are some fairy tales. But if Krishna wants, He can have billions of boars coming out of the nose of Lord Brahma.

Why is He restricted by time and space or by measurements? Why should God be under any kind of measurement? It's actually ludicrous to put God under any kind of measurement because then you're contradicting yourself completely. You're saying that God should be the creator, so if He's the creator then surely He created laws? And if He created laws, why would He be under them? And if He's not under them, surely He should do things that are beyond the laws of nature? And if He does do things that are beyond the laws of nature, then we say, 'Oh, it's mythological!' This is our vision.

Therefore, one has to hear from the *acaryas*, the great devotees, *mahajanas*. One has to hear directly from *Srimad Bhagavatam* and *Bhagavad-gita*.

In the *Bhagavad-gita*, Krishna says, *mayadhyaksena prakrti suyate sa - caracaram*, 'Within the material energy, both the moving and non-moving, the animate and inanimate are working under My direction'. No one in the history of mankind has ever said that. Did Jesus Christ say this whole universe is working under my direction? Did Mohammed? None of them. Krishna is the only person known in the history of mankind that said, 'All of these universes sprout from Me, and I am the creator'. And He wasn't shy to speak it. He spoke it repeatedly on the battlefield of Kuruksetra to Arjuna. He repeated it over and over again. *Aham sarvasya prabhavo*. In so many verses. He used the word, *aham* – I am. What do the impersonalists say? 'Oh, He didn't mean *Him*, He meant the unborn, unmanifested, unspoken, untouchable within Him'. What right have they got to add that? Do they think Krishna is in need of their added speculation? How dare they try to do that? Do they think that Krishna left something out to be opinionated by them? Do they think they're greater than God, that they should add something to God's words? God comes to the material world but He's so pathetic that He can't speak properly? So I needed to come along and write what He really meant.

Krishna says, *bhoktaram yajna tapasam sarva loka mahesvaram*, 'I am the supreme controller and the supreme enjoyer of all the universes'. Nobody is saying that, and yet Krishna was a person.

Throughout all of the Vedic literature, He is established as the Supreme Person. But they want to somehow nullify this individuality of God because it's incomprehensible to their tiny pea-brain that God can be an individual supreme person and yet be the controller. And even more wonderful is that Krishna can come and become completely submissive to His devotees in His form as the son of Mother Yasoda and King Nanda. That same Supreme Personality of Godhead who is manifesting billions and billions of universes and planets and energies has become a child in the courtyard of Nanda.

Therefore, the devotee is saying, 'I should worship Nanda Maharaja, because he has God playing in his courtyard. You want to understand God, but Nanda Maharaja has God bringing Nanda's slippers on His head. Therefore the *vaisnavas* worship the devotees because the devotees have captured Krishna. Krishna is *acyuta* and *adhoksaja,* beyond any jurisdiction of senses, beyond any conceivability of the mind, beyond everything. And yet He is captured in the courtyard of Nanda Maharaja.

So here, the very prayer is suggesting that God is sentient and can hear prayers and fulfil the desires of the devotee. We have to understand, what is sentience? That is the whole study in the Vedic literature. Modern scientists have completely ridiculous ideas of what consciousness is. They think it is some sort of chemical combination or some sort of material interaction. And yet we see they are unable to create consciousness. There are billions upon trillions of ants. They can't even create one ant. And even if they could, what's the big deal? There are billions upon billions of them. They can only talk about their so-called observations of ants and their speculations of how the energies are working. They can't understand how the energy of Krishna works.

Krishna is *sat cit ananda vigraha*, the form of eternity, knowledge and bliss. That is the description of pure sentience. Bliss and knowledge are two things which we need essentially in our lives. First of all, we need knowledge as it means consciousness. There's no separation between consciousness and knowledge. As soon as you are conscious you take in knowledge, you absorb certain types of information. You are seeing, hearing, smelling, touching and tasting all of the time. These knowledge-acquiring senses are there because one is in great need of knowledge.

At the moment, that knowledge is not there because we are in a desert-like atmosphere. In the desert you need water, but there's very little available so it's a big endeavour to find it. If you were in the desert, what would you be doing? You'd be looking for water. The fact that you're constantly looking for water indicates that perhaps there's no water there. Because if there was water readily available you wouldn't be looking for it.

Similarly, the material world is full of ignorance. We are always looking for knowledge. That means you're an ignoramus, a fool, an idiot, a twit. What are all the words they have? Thickhead, twit, fool, ignoramus, spud-head, moron, dope-head, brick-head, idiot. Why? Because that is our nature in the material world. Considering the fact that we are constantly searching for knowledge but no one can see the simple fact, that the reason we are searching for it is that we don't have it.

We spend our whole lifetime questioning because the material world is so limited and imperfect that we are always trying to ascertain some mastership over it. We need mastership and knowledge to get a certain degree of control. Just like, unless you know how to cook, the kitchen is useless. The kitchen is only valuable when you have knowledge. You may have so many nice pots and pans and everything. But if you don't know how to cook, what is the use? So the material is only useful when you know how to use it. Knowledge is not there automatically, we have to acquire it.

Another aspect of spirit is bliss, *ananda*. So these three things if you study them very carefully you'll find they are the constitution of the soul, eternity, knowledge and finally bliss. We want to have that bliss. If you are in an empty room with just four walls, how long can you stand there for? Not very long until you become disturbed because our nature is that we will search for variety. One will have to have some varieties, some variegatedness will have to be there. Therefore enjoyment means two. It has to be two, isn't it? You and something else. Whether that something else is food, association with another person or going somewhere, whatever it is, there's always me and variegatedness.

This variegatedness is the source of our pleasure. In the material world, everyone is very much desirous of creating a state of happiness by creating a certain environment. And within that environment, we try to have our pleasures. That's because the nature of the soul is to be a person. A person means personality, and personality means variegatedness. Each individual person is recognised by his individual variegatedness. We are all individual people and we have different propensities, thoughts, ideas and natures. Not everyone is doing the same thing.

Therefore, the quality of variety has to be studied because that is our individual, intrinsic nature coming from the soul. The body is just simply dead, inanimate matter but as soon as consciousness is there, variety is there. How is it difficult to understand that God is the reservoir of all variety? He is the reservoir of all variegatedness. All variegatedness rests in Him. Because He is the creator of everything. It would be ridiculous to say that variegatedness is in His creation but not in Him as well. It's ludicrous. Because Krishna is *acintya bhedabheda tattva*, simultaneously one and different from this creation.

Therefore by His creation, one can get some inkling of understanding how variegated God's mind is. From Him many wonderful arrangements emanate. And even the energy we're observing is the inferior energy. Just imagine if you went to visit Birmingham prison without seeing the rest of Birmingham, you only saw the inside of the prison and you were awestruck, dumbfounded, amazed at just seeing one little cell within the prison, then what to speak of what the city must be like. If that's what the prison looks like, imagine what the city looks like. In America, they have hi-tech prisons. It's a very big and rich country, so the prison is also wealthy. But if you go to a poor country, the prison is just an old hole and they stick you down there. If this material world is like a prison, imagine what the spiritual world is like.

Ravi: You were talking about the point that if God can't be a person then you are limiting God. But can God create a person who is greater than Him? Could He create a person who was a superior and more powerful creator? Not that just He could be conquered only by love, but by a person superior in potency.

Tribhuvanatha: Yes Krishna *does* do that. Krishna has *advaitam acyutam anadim ananta rupam*. The Lord is always expanding in greater and greater ways. Krishna is in Vrindavan, but at the same time, Vishnu is creating all of the variegated universes and expansions - *Vasudeva, Sankarsana, Pradyumna, Aniruddha* etc. In that sense, one could say that the forms of Vishnu are in one sense greater than Vishnu. In the Vedic literature, Vishnu is described as the source of incarnations. We say God is unlimited because He has unlimited expansions. Each of those expansions has a role according to His desire. Sometimes He comes in one expansion and fights when He comes in the material world.

It's kind of a moot question because everything is God. Whatever God does, it's still God. You're also God but you're a very tiny God. He's created you. Suppose Krishna created a person called Roger that's going to be greater than Him, but that's still Krishna called Roger. He's still Krishna. Spirit is not: one minus one is nothing. Krishna is Krishna and everything is Krishna. Therefore whatever Krishna does is still Krishna. Even if it's greater than Krishna, it's still Krishna. So there's no question that Krishna can't create something better than Krishna because everything is Krishna anyway. He just has expansions and energies. That is the meaning of God.

13: SPIRITUAL ENERGY DOESN'T WORK UNDER CONDITIONS

A TALK AT ISKCON IN BIRMINGHAM, UK - 1997

Krishna says, 'When I come to the material world fools think that I am born under certain conditions, and that I function under certain conditions, but they do not know My transcendental nature and My supreme dominion over all that be'. They don't understand that. It's very difficult for people to understand that Krishna has dominion over everything because He was a 'body'. I have been trying for 30 years and I don't even have dominion over my wife or my children - let alone my body. In actuality, I have no dominion over my body, sometimes it does very embarrassing things and there's nothing I can do about it. I have to sit there and watch. So an intelligent person can understand that we don't even have dominion over our bodies. But then we think, 'Krishna has come as a body. He must be like me. I feel very sad for Him. He also was born like me'.

There's a story of when Nehru, the prime minister of India, visited a mental asylum. He was having a tour of the facilities and he met one person who he thought seemed to be very normal and intelligent.
'What are you doing here?', Nehru said, 'You seem like a very intelligent guy'.
He appeared to be fine, there was nothing wrong with him.
The man just looked at him and said,
'You shouldn't be here, you're too clever!'
Nehru said to him, 'Do you know who I am? Do you know who you are talking to?'
And the guy said, 'No'.
Then Nehru said, 'I am Nehru, the prime minister'.
And the man said, '*Shh*, don't say that too loud'.
Nehru said, 'No, it's true!'.
The guy said, 'Don't say that, that's why I'm in here!'

So, the fool considers that, 'This person Krishna, He was like me! He was chasing after young girls in the forest! I like to do that as well. I like to run after girls in the forest. Who doesn't like to run after beautiful girls in the forest?' Yes, that is the nature. Everyone likes to have lots of riches and wealth and they think that 'Krishna has come to this world and He is in need of these things too. He has to have a palace and a wife'. They think He is in need.

There is a nice pastime at the *Rajasuya* sacrifice ceremony of Maharaja Yudhisthira. King Yudhisthira nominated Krishna as the principal guest, the chief guest who presides over the *yajna* (fire ceremony). But Sisupala objected, 'This Krishna! He should not be the honoured guest in this assembly! He was found in the Vrindavan forest dancing with so many young girls late at night! Did you know that?' It was like some new gossip, he was giving the daily news report. So then the whole assembly was listening attentively to Sisupala, and then Bhismadeva spoke up. Bhismadeva was a *naisthika brahmacari,* a celibate monk, he never passed semen in his life. Bhismadeva stood up and said, 'Well, I have been a *brahmacari* all of my life! One would consider nominating me as the chief guest, but I nominate Krishna because although He was in the forest late at night with so many *gopis* (young cowherd girls), He was never agitated, not once!'

When Krishna comes to the material world, He does not come here like you. You come here because you are inadequate and you need to enjoy sense gratification. That's why you need a body. If you're not given a body, you've got no sense gratification. The only reason you can enjoy anything is that you've been given it. If you've been given eyeballs, you can see. If you have no eyeballs, you can't see - simple. Whatever you have been given, that's what allows you to act. Certain creatures see under certain conditions but if the body is not favourable, then your experience of sense gratification cannot be favourable. That means invalid. When we have a body that is not perfectly situated it becomes invalid. For what? Sense gratification. The body is given to you because you need you're vitally in need of *ananda* or happiness. We need to enjoy *ananda*.

We want to eat very nice foods. We need delicious curd *sabjis* with thick cream. We need it. We vitally need it. We need to enjoy nice perfumes and smells. We need to hear people say nice things about us, about how wonderful we are, how handsome and pretty we are, how intelligent we are, how advanced we are. We need that vitally. We need all of these things. We need to see beautiful things like nice scenery. People are flying all over the world to see something, they want to see the pyramids of Egypt or the jungles of Africa. They are flying here and there. They are going to the movies because they want to see something. They have to have videos and televisions because they are vitally in need of seeing. They want to hear nice music and they sit for hours. There's a sound system that the speakers alone cost one hundred thousand pounds each. I have a friend who sells them. For two speakers, it would be two hundred thousand pounds and he has many customers. They are hi-fi addicts. We need to hear. We want to hear the sweet tidings of our consort. 'Oh my *guchy wuchy*, you're so nice! You're so strong, handsome, and intelligent. You have such big muscles.' And the girl wants to hear, 'Oh you're the prettiest thing I have seen in my life'. We want to hear that. And she says, 'Oh really? You think like that?'

We are in need, so we think that if God comes, He must also be in need. They don't know He's God so they think that Krishna has come in need. Krishna says, 'These foolish people do not understand My transcendental nature' because Krishna is covered by His curtain of *maya*. If you have a curtain on stage, you can't see what's behind the stage. There could be a whole arrangement behind the curtain but it's not until it opens that you can say, 'Oh look, isn't that wonderful!' Sometimes everyone is sitting in the theatre, and the curtains are closed. Everyone is sitting anxiously wondering, 'What is behind that curtain?'

Similarly, when Krishna comes He has His curtain of *yogamaya*. He is covered by that curtain so that those who try to make Krishna an object of their sense gratification will never be able to approach Him. Krishna can never be an object of your sense gratification. Everyone wants everything to be an object of their sense gratification. Why are movie stars paid high salaries? Because they're an object of sense gratification. People want to see them, so they pay money to see them. They are big movie stars, but they have to rehearse their lines and they have to go in front of the cameras. They have to be at certain promotions. They have to do so many things to satisfy their masters. Their masters are their paymasters. So they're an object of sense gratification. They are servants of their fans and adorers. But Krishna is not like that. Krishna does not have to do anything. He can never become subjugated by the tiny living entity. The living entity in the material world can never subjugate God to do anything. As He says in the *Bhagavad-gita aham sarvasya prabhavo*, 'I am the Master of this material energy. This material energy is working under My dominion'.

mayadhyaksena prakrti suyate sacaracaram
hetunanena kaunteya jagat viparivartate (Bhagavad-gita 9.10)

'All of this material energy is working under My direction. I am the one who produces all moving and non-moving beings'. *Bija 'ham*, Krishna says, 'I am the seed of everything. I am the seed of existence'. This arrangement of the material energy is simply the sport of God. Krishna comes here to play. Everything is Krishna's playground. Krishna comes to the material world to play and enjoy. He exhibits His internal potency and shows how He is the Supreme Enjoyer. Therefore people say, 'Oh mythological! 16,108 wives? Who could have that many wives? Have you ever tried to have that many wives? Even if you have five wives you would go mad, even with two or three. One is enough'. So Krishna had 16,108 wives and He gave each one a beautiful palace. 'Oh, how can He do that? Even for one wife, I had to save all my life to get a house and we still haven't paid for it. We are still struggling with the arrears. How can this Krishna do it?'

Krishna has a problem because if He does anything extraordinary, people say, 'Oh! Mythological stories!' Fantasy stories. Stories about fairy tales and mythological creatures! Like out of the Greek epics. And if Krishna doesn't do anything, if He simply gets a job in the labour exchange, then no one will be impressed. Suppose someone told the story that - Krishna was born, He got a job driving a chariot, and then He got another job but He got refused because He didn't have a good enough education. People would ask, 'What did Krishna do that was so special?' If He comes here and does nothing people will criticize, 'What is that? Nothing special! Why should He be God?'

Even Sai Baba has to do something. He can't say, 'I'm God' and then do nothing. He has to produce a little gold now and again, or some ashes, or appear in a picture. He has to do something otherwise you might say, 'What has he done?' Any type of so-called God in the world, they've all got to do something. But all of these so-called Gods that have come in the last one thousand years have any of them shown their universal form? Have any of them spoken the *Bhagavad-gita*? Where do we see any of them producing such knowledge as the *Bhagavad-gita*?

If you study Krishna very carefully you will see that He is supreme in every aspect. Krishna is supreme in knowledge. He is the supreme lover. He is the supreme autocrat or King. He is the supreme warrior. He is the supreme renouncer. No one can be more renounced than Krishna. No one is purer than Krishna. There is no one more intelligent than Krishna. Nobody who has come to this world is more powerful than Krishna. We don't have any example in the history of mankind greater than Krishna. Do you know anyone who had 16,108 wives? Do you see it in the Guinness Book of World Records? Maybe someone came after Krishna and had 16,208 wives with all their palaces fully equipped with diamonds, jewels and marble, having a luxurious life. Every queen was living life aristocratically and each one had ten children.

That's a lot of children! Imagine if you had to buy them all a set of shoes. You would be shopping for a long time. What to speak of feeding them. But Krishna is feeding billions of living entities. He is feeding so many elephants in the jungle. He is feeding birds. He is looking after everyone. Krishna can have sixteen billion wives and each one of them can live on their own planet and it will be no problem.

Om purnam adah purnam idam. Krishna is *purnam,* complete. There is no inconsistency in God. There is no incompleteness or inadequacy in God. The display of Krishna in the material world is only a tiny display. Krishna says to Arjuna in the *Bhagavad-gita,* 'Whatever you see is only a tiny spark of My splendour. Behold My mystic opulence'. He maintains the entire creation with one small particle of His energy. In the material world if you minus one from one, it leaves nothing. If you take one from one in the spiritual plane, one is still there. If a million universes come out of the body of Krishna there is still another one million.

Purnam means everything. He is the complete whole, even though so many universes emanate from Him, He remains the complete balance. He is the complete because He is sufficiently capable of supporting everything. We cannot support even our own bodies. We struggle for our whole life to support one miserable body and keep it going. Just to keep it fed, alive and happy is such a struggle. And yet, Krishna can support trillions of universes, without even disturbing His mealtime. Krishna is enjoying in Goloka eating delicious foodstuffs. He is not disturbed even with the cowherd boys. He is enjoying. *Go* means senses. *Govinda* means 'One who gives complete pleasure to the senses'. The planet of Goloka is for giving pleasure to Krishna's senses.

When Krishna comes to the material world He never goes past the age of sixteen. N*avayauvanam* means Krishna never gets old. You don't see any pictures of Krishna with an old man's beard and a walking stick. Wherever you see Krishna, He is a beaming youth. *Govindam adi purusam*, Krishna is ever-youthful. In this world, things deteriorate with age, but we like fresh things. We buy fresh food, not rotten food. We like everything to be fresh but in the material world, everything becomes influenced by time. It becomes rotten and stinking. Just like you buy milk and the next day it becomes rotten and stinky, so you have to throw it away. In the material world, things are only apparently fresh, but they are not fresh because they're made up of an inferior constitution. The material body is made up of an inferior substance, therefore it decays very quickly.

Dehino 'smin yatha dehe kaumaram yauvanam jara tatha dehantara praptir dhiras tatra na muhyati. Krishna says, 'the embodied soul continuously passes, in this body, from boyhood to youth to old age'. We have nice bodies when we are young, but when we are middle-aged, we get a bit *roly-poly*, a bit fat. Then we gradually start getting old. Everyone goes through it. When you are young, you laugh at the old but when you are old, the youth are laughing at you.

Prabhupada told a story that in India they have dry cow dung patties. They put the fresh cow dung on the side of the wall and it gradually dries. When it's dry you can use it for the fire. So the wet cow dung is laughing at the dry cow dung, '*Ha ha*, you're going to go in the fire today'. But it doesn't know that in a very short time it will become dry and then also go in the fire. So all of us, we will end up in the fire of the material world. Or we will get fed to the worms and give them an extra meal when they run out of vegetables. Worms in graveyards are the happiest creatures because they get lots of bodies put in there all the time to have a good meal.

Don't think that when Krishna comes, He has such a body. We have to study Krishna as the Supreme Personality of Godhead. 'Behold My transcendental body, behold My transcendental power, behold My transcendental opulence, behold My transcendental beauty, behold My transcendental name'. He is coming to show us this fact, but we have no interest. We are too busy chasing after other bodies. If you see how people are busy-bodies chasing after other bodies, they say, 'Oh, I don't have time for reading *Bhagavad-gita*. I'm too busy with my body! I am busy with my other bodies! Little baby bodies, mummy bodies and daddy bodies'.

So people don't have any time to study Krishna's body. But if you study Krishna, then you will understand all other bodies. All other bodies are created by Krishna. Just like with the sun in the sky, everything else comes into proper perspective. Otherwise, we are grovelling in the dark. Just like these philosophers they are looking and studying the world. Freud - or fraud - is studying the body. 'Oh this is the reason - we are all animals, monkeys, chasing after sex.' But why don't you study Krishna's body? Then you will understand all other bodies. All other bodies come by Krishna's arrangement. Krishna creates the material body and also the spiritual body.

We have to understand that Krishna is *sat cit ananda vigraha*:

Sat means eternal, fully competent. It doesn't just mean eternal. It means that there is no inadequacy, totally complete. Everybody wants adequacy, not inadequacy. In the material world, everything is *asat*. *Asat* means fully inadequate. *Sat* means fully adequate.

Cit means full of consciousness. This body is not full of consciousness. The body is unconscious. You chop your arm off and it's useless. What would be the use of walking around with a dead arm? You can say that the arm is a very nice thing but would you like carrying a few in your pocket? If someone saw you walking down the road with a bunch of arms, 'Well, I only had two but now I've got eight!' What is the use of a dead arm? But when it is connected with consciousness it is so useful. Consciousness is the superior arrangement. That transcendental body is *cit,* full of consciousness. Skin and bones and veins and pumps and machines and organs: Krishna's body is not like that.

Ananda means full of transcendental pleasure, not misery. Everything here is *nirananda,* the opposite of pleasure. *A-brahma-bhuvanat lokah,* Krishna says, 'From the highest planet to the lowest they are all places of misery wherein repeated birth and death take place'. So we have to transfer ourselves to the plane of transcendental bliss, *ananda mayo'bhyasat*. Therefore Krishna comes and says, 'This is the plane where you belong - in My plane'. He comes down from the highest plane to this plane to show us, here is Vaikuntha. This is what it looks like.

Lord Caitanya comes and shows us how to capture Vaikuntha. Krishna shows it but not everyone sees it because they are very unfortunate. Krishna says, 'First you surrender then I will allow you unto that plane'. But people aren't ready to surrender. 'No, no, I have no time! I have so many responsibilities! I want to stay here. Things are going to get better here. A new prime minister is here with a new government. They are going to make sure we solve all of our problems. They are going to install telephones and radios and televisions and so many gadgetries, so we are all going to get happy and live happily ever after'. They have no interest. So then Lord Caitanya comes and shows what that plane of Krishna consciousness is. Therefore it is called Caitanya Caritamrta: that plane of *amrita,* nectar. Everybody wants *amrita*. But they are looking on that wrong plane. They are looking on the material plane for *amrita*. But He is saying, 'No, you can get this *amrita* simply by chanting:

Hare Krishna Hare Krishna   Krishna Krishna Hare Hare
Hare Rama Hare Rama   Rama Rama Hare Hare

It is very simple. Transfer yourself by sound. The transcendental sound can elevate you like an aeroplane. When you want to go to another country, you transfer yourself by sitting on a plane and floating on the airwaves. Similarly, you can sit in the transcendental sound. It is so powerful that it can carry the whole universe in it. And you can be transferred to the spiritual Goloka by this chanting.

Lord Caitanya came just in case anyone wasn't convinced to show by practical demonstration the effect of chanting Hare Krishna. When Krishna came He didn't do that. Krishna's business isn't to be the servant of anyone. Lord

Caitanya has come as the servant of everyone. Krishna's business is to demand, 'Surrender, you rogues and thieves! You're all a bunch of thieves stealing from Me! Do you want to give it up? Then come to me!' Krishna's *avatar* form of Lord Caitanya is so kind that to the biggest thieves He says, 'Look, My dear friend. You simply add Krishna, the chanting of Hare Krishna and then you will get the mercy'.

Ananta Nitai: You were speaking about the negative side of temporality. But when we see the artists of this world produce something it only happens once and therefore it is temporary, but still, it's unique. Something unique is superior because it isn't reproducible. Things like art and music are temporary but they're also unique and beautiful. So why is it bad if things are temporary? Why is temporality a bad thing?

Tribhuvanatha: So it uniquely doesn't last. That makes it unique?

Ananta Nitai: It might be temporary but it's still unique.

Tribhuvanatha: No, I can understand your point, but what is the use? If you have a plate of food and it disappears before you eat it - that's very unique. People will be amazed. Every time you go to eat it - it disappears. But how many people would come into your restaurant? Suppose you open a restaurant and every time you go to eat, it disappears. Everyone will come to see it, but no one will get very fat.

Something disappears, yes, it's wonderful. In this world, everything disappears. Even the planets disappear. This is the world of disappearing. You will also disappear. You're sitting here now but you will disappear. I will disappear. We all will disappear. So yes, many things in this world are wonderful, but everything is disappearing. Just like when there is an aeroplane crash, three hundred people disappear into the ocean. It's on the front page news, 'Today three hundred people disappeared!' It's hard to get rid of three hundred people, isn't it? But they were there and then where did they go?

So, everything is disappearing, but disappearing isn't very nice. It may be fascinating to the mind but it's not the cause of pleasure. It only gives pleasure when Krishna disappears, there is *vipralambha*, love in separation. But generally disappearing means sadness. Just like when you have a child and it falls in the water… gone! Everyone is fascinated, 'Oh, where did that child go?' But you are crying! Your heart is broken! 'Oh, where is my child? Disappeared! Where's my wife? Disappeared! Where are all my lovers? They're all gone! Disappeared!'

In the material world, everyone is trying to make things appear but everything is disappearing. I want to find a nice situation, but suddenly it disappears. 'I wanted a nice wife, but she disappeared… with the milkman… and took all my money!' Everything is disappearing in front of you, including your body. Every molecule in your body, every cell is disappearing, disintegrating in front of your very eyes. Look in the mirror every ten years, but one year you won't look into it anymore. The mirror will still be there but you won't be looking in it because you would have disappeared.

Ananta Nitai: But if there weren't any changes, it'd be worse.

Tribhuvanatha: It'd be worse? It'd be more boring, would it? If we all stay around forever?

Ananta Nitai: Yes, exactly!

Tribhuvanatha: Maybe it's better that we all disappear. That just shows you how inferior this energy is. You're better off without it. If it stays around too long… You see that when people come and visit you. Sometimes you think, 'I hope they don't stay around too long. These guys will eat me out of house and home'. So what do you do? You try to make it more unfriendly for them. 'Oh, I ran out of food today! There's no hot water. I'm sorry I'd like to give you a drink but we've got nothing in stock!'

In India, there is the story of a man who wanted to arrange for his daughters to get married. He got them all married, one by one, but he was so wealthy that they all started living in his house. He thought, 'My goodness! This is getting out of control! How do I get rid of them?' So every day he removed one item from the cooking. If there was a vegetable, he took it away. Then the next day, another vegetable. And the next day the rice went. So gradually as things were disappearing, the guys were thinking, 'I've got to get out of here or we are going to starve to death'. So one by one each couple started moving away. But there was one last one who stuck it out until there was only salt every day. So the father thought, 'This man is never going to go!' So he beat him on the head with a shoe, 'Get out of here!' And chased him out of the door.

That's the way we are in the material world. We are getting beaten. One minute this goes, then that goes, and we are trying to bring it back. When you get old, you lose your potency for sex, so now they have drugs that even at eighty years of age, you can get excited. They think this is bringing it back! Somehow it's gone, but bring it back! What they can't do is stop old age. Old age will take everyone away. Everyone is disappearing. And it's true - if we stuck around too long, we would definitely be unwanted guests. We are not wanted here. We are not wanted. Nobody wants anybody. The parents bring you up but when they are old, in these countries nowadays they stick them in a home. 'Get them out of the way, quick! They'll get in the way of the kids'.

We are not wanted here. Neither does anyone want us to be here, nor do we want to be here. So better to move on, we think. But actually what spiritual life means is better to move to Vaikuntha. Here we have moved from one apartment to another, from one body to another, simply different types of pleasure and different types of pain. But spiritual life means to get out of this plane. Why should I be content with such an inferior arrangement? Why should I tolerate such a situation? That's actual intelligence.

Just like these people, they are not tolerating. 'Why should we tolerate? Zero tolerance!' The politician is preaching, 'Get rid of poverty! Get rid of disease! Get rid of all these problems!' 'Oh wonderful, wonderful, we will elect him next time. He'll do better than the other guy. The other guy was useless, he promises loads of things, and gives nothing. This guy, he's even good looking. He is sure to be able to deliver the goods!'

And then after a while, 'Get rid of him! Bring in another'. Our dear Maggie Thatcher, when she first started, she was so popular. 'Maggie will sort things out!' And now everyone is complaining. At the time of her election, they were praising her, but now they are grumpy. These things have been going on, since time immemorial. When Srila Prabhupada was in France, there was a statue of Napoleon and under the statue, it was written, 'There is no France without Napoleon', and Prabhupada said, 'Where is Napoleon? France is still there but what happened to Napoleon?'

That's the reality of life. We might try to make a nice cosy situation but in reality, we are just simply actors appearing for our little performance. We've all done our little performance and we all go out. We all bow out, flat. As it says in the Bible we are dead bodies flapping for a few days. Our bodies are dead and we may flap them around and everyone thinks, 'Oh look at that, a nice body flapping'. One day they will all fall. Don't take shelter of this material body, take shelter of a spiritual body. If you want to take shelter of a spiritual body then you have to chant:

Hare Krishna Hare Krishna   Krishna Krishna Hare Hare
Hare Rama Hare Rama   Rama Rama Hare Hare

'O Arjuna, as the Supreme Personality of Godhead, I know everything that has happened in the past, all that is happening in the present, and all things that are yet to come. I also know all living entities, but Me no one knows'.
That is God. Nobody knows God. That's the difference.

14: THE BEAUTY OF SRILA PRABHUPADA

I was just contemplating that in the material world everyone strives for perfection. The natural inclination of consciousness is towards perfection, and one of the biggest disappointments of the material world is that it's not perfect. I remember that as a young idealistic person, I was very much searching after some sort of meaning to life, to the point that I gave up almost all connection with everything. And I think that one of the beautiful things of coming in touch with Krishna consciousness was that I saw there was a perfect philosophy.

Of course, having a perfect philosophy doesn't necessarily mean it can be appreciated by an imperfect person. There's always this difficulty that even if something is perfect, we are not perfect, therefore, we cannot appreciate it adequately. Even though this philosophy has been there in India for thousands of years and has been read by hundreds of thousands of people, the difference is that to understand the perfect philosophy you have to meet the perfect person. Philosophy alone is only intellectualism.

One of the beauties of meeting Srila Prabhupada was that I saw he was a completely perfect person. And every single moment of association I had with Prabhupada confirmed that perfection. When we see a perfect person, sometimes we think of perfection in terms of material quality, but the beauty of Srila Prabhupada was that he was perfect both materially and spiritually. He had all of the wonderful qualities of being aristocratic, intelligent and unconquerable. Prabhupada was never defeated by anyone in any field of discussion. I never once saw Prabhupada stumble in anything he did.

He apparently had complete control of the material energy and I and many others would say they have studied Prabhupada deeply. To study the spiritual master is not bad because Srila Prabhupada was a living, perfect pure devotee. We could see in every single aspect, he was perfect. One of the most impressive things about Srila Prabhupada's perfection was that he had complete love for Krishna. One of the beauties of our life in Krishna consciousness is that Krishna is always very mercifully showing our inadequacies and how to improve, and this is very nice and we should be very grateful for that.

Once when we were on a morning walk with Srila Prabhupada a devotee said to him, 'I don't remember one single pious thing I have done', and Srila Prabhupada stopped, put his cane on the ground, looked him in the eyes and said, 'I am your pious activity'. So I thought that was such a beautiful answer because I myself have also never done anything pious. And all of us should always remember how he sacrificed his life to help us and help others.

ABOUT THE AUTHOR

Tribhuvanatha dasa (born Thomas Kevin Hegarty) appeared in this world in 1952. He was born in Longford, Ireland. Despite many serious challenges in his upbringing he was noted for his determination and his forbearance amidst the difficulties he faced. He was always known to be a very discerning person with a deep capacity to tolerate trying circumstances. In 1968, at the age of 16, he left home to work in London, trying to make a life for himself there.

In 1969 he encountered the Hare Krishna Movement and started practising and studying Krishna consciousness, *bhakti yoga*. He was an astute student with a very logical and analytical mind. He quickly became very expert at understanding and explaining the ancient Vedic texts such as the *Bhagavad Gita, Isopanisad* and the *Srimad Bhagavatam (Bhagavata Purana)*.

Shortly after joining the Krishna consciousness movement and the Radha Krishna Temple *ashram* in London, he met the founder, Prabhupada, whom he immediately accepted as his spiritual master.

Overwhelmed by the genuine spiritual love given to him and his fellow community members by Srila Prabhupada, he accepted initiation from His Divine Grace A.C. Bhaktivedanta Swami Prabhupada, formally becoming his disciple in 1970. Thus Srila Prabhupada became his life's inspiration.

As a full-time member of the International Society for Krishna Consciousness he helped to share Bhakti yoga with people around the world. He was instrumental in opening new projects and temples in the UK at a time when the ancient Vedic culture was not familiar to people.

Although his early education had not been elaborate, he soon became a well-renowned and respected spiritual leader, scholar and musician. By the grace of his *guru* he quickly learnt whatever he needed and was invited to speak at many events and major universities around the world.

He spent the majority of his life as a monk and was appreciated for his personal touch in his caring and philosophical guidance on real-life issues. He travelled to many countries in the world inspiring people with his talks and his singing of *kirtan* (devotional mantra music). He was instrumental in the opening of temples, cultural centres and farm projects in the United Kingdom, Ireland and in East Africa, thereby changing the lives of thousands of people. He participated in the opening of eco-farms and rural non-profit spiritual projects and was also a major influence in the opening of spiritual orphanages in Africa where the children get a home and an education both in spiritual and material knowledge. In other words, his life's mission was to serve Krishna and to serve others on their journey in life.

In the last few years of his life, he encountered serious health difficulties, being diagnosed with cancer, but his spirit shone greater than ever. He explained that he was not fearful but grateful and said that death is comparable to a changing of dress and that the soul is eternal. He left his body in 2001 at the age of 48. Many people around the world take him as a *guru* or a spiritually inspirational figure. He credited all of his life's successes to his spiritual master, Srila Prabhupada.

ABOUT SRILA PRABHUPADA

His Divine Grace A.C. Bhaktivedanta Swami Prabhupada appeared in this world in 1896 in Calcutta, India. He first met his spiritual master, Srila Bhaktisiddhanta Sarasvati Goswami, in Calcutta in 1922. Bhaktisiddhanta Sarasvati, a prominent intellectual and spiritual leader in India, liked this educated young man and convinced him to dedicate his life to teaching Vedic knowledge. Srila Prabhupada became his student and, in 1933, his formally initiated disciple. At their first meeting Srila Bhaktisiddhanta Sarasvati requested Srila Prabhupada to broadcast Vedic knowledge in English. In the years that followed, Srila Prabhupada wrote a commentary on the Bhagavad-gita, assisted the Gaudiya Math in its work, and, in 1944, started *Back to Godhead*, an English fortnightly magazine. Single-handedly, Srila Prabhupada typed the manuscripts, edited, checked the galley proofs, and even distributed the individual copies. The magazine is now being continued by his disciples in the West.

In 1950 Srila Prabhupada retired from married life, adopting the *vanaprastha* (retired) order to devote more time to his studies and writing. He travelled to the holy city of Vrindavan, where he lived in humble circumstances in the historic temple of Radha-Damodara. There he engaged for several years in deep study and writing. He accepted the renounced order of life (*sannyasa*) in 1959. At Radha-Damodara, Srila Prabhupada began work on his life's masterpiece: a multivolume commentated translation of the eighteen thousand verse *Srimad-Bhagavatam (Bhagavata Purana)*. He also wrote *Easy Journey to Other Planets*.

After publishing three volumes of the *Bhagavatam*, Srila Prabhupada came to the United States, in September 1965, to fulfil the mission of his spiritual master. Subsequently, His Divine Grace wrote more than fifty volumes of authoritative commentated translations and summary studies of the philosophical and religious classics of India.

142

When he first arrived by freighter in New York City, Srila Prabhupada was practically penniless. Only after almost a year of great difficulty did he establish the International Society for Krishna consciousness, in July of 1966. Before he passed away on November 14, 1977, he had guided the Society and seen it grow to a worldwide confederation of more than one hundred ashrams, schools, temples, institutes, and farm communities.

Srila Prabhupada also inspired the construction of several large international cultural centres in India. In Sridham Mayapur a spiritual city has been constructed. In Vrindavan are the magnificent Krishna-Balarama Temple and International Guesthouse, *gurukula* school, and Srila Prabhupada Memorial and Museum. There is also a major cultural and educational centre in Bombay. Major centres are located in Delhi and in a dozen other important locations on the Indian subcontinent.

Srila Prabhupada's most significant contribution, however, is his books. Highly respected by scholars for their authority, depth, and clarity, they are used as textbooks in numerous college courses. His writings have been translated into over fifty languages. The Bhaktivedanta Book Trust, established in 1972 to publish the works of His Divine Grace, has thus become the world's largest publisher of books in the field of Indian religion and philosophy. Over half a billion of his books have been printed in dozens of languages. Making them the most widely read books on eastern wisdom of the last fifty years.

In just twelve years, despite his advanced age, Srila Prabhupada circled the globe fourteen times on lecture tours that took him to six continents. Yet this vigorous schedule did not slow his prolific literary output. His writings constitute a veritable library of Vedic philosophy, religion, literature, and culture.

The books of Srila Prabhupada are highly recommended, especially 'Bhagavad Gita as it is' and 'The Science of Self-Realisation'.